Mind Energy

The Power of ME!

Timothy M. Ferris

iUniverse, Inc.
New York   Bloomington

Mind Energy
The Power of ME!

Copyright © 2010 by Timothy M. Ferris

All rights reserved. No part of this book may be used or reproduced by any means, graphic, electronic, or mechanical, including photocopying, recording, taping or by any information storage retrieval system without the written permission of the publisher except in the case of brief quotations embodied in critical articles and reviews.

The views expressed in this work are solely those of the author and do not necessarily reflect the views of the publisher, and the publisher hereby disclaims any responsibility for them.

iUniverse books may be ordered through booksellers or by contacting:

iUniverse
1663 Liberty Drive
Bloomington, IN 47403
www.iuniverse.com
1-800-Authors (1-800-288-4677)

Because of the dynamic nature of the Internet, any Web addresses or links contained in this book may have changed since publication and may no longer be valid.

ISBN: 978-1-4502-5774-9 (sc)
ISBN: 978-1-4502-5775-6 (dj)
ISBN: 978-1-4502-5776-3 (ebk)

Library of Congress Control Number: 2010913321

Printed in the United States of America

iUniverse rev. date: 9/21/2010

Contents

Acknowledgements vii

Foreward ix

Section 1: Preparing Yourself for Success 1
Who Are You Now and Who Will You Be In The Future? . . . 3
  Imagine the Possibilities!
The Time To Create Your Future Is Now 9
  Thought Linked to Purpose Becomes Creative Force
Understanding the Silent Killer of Success: 17
  Simple Methods for Recognizing and Breaking Through
  Procrastination
The Past Does Not Equal The Future 27
  Who You Are Today Does Not Control Who You Can
  Become

Section 2: Creating a Compelling Future Step-By-Step . 37
Defining Your Life's Purpose and Creating a Life Plan 39
  Discovering What's Important To You
Developing Compelling Goals That Support Your Life Plan   47
  Ask and It Will Be Given To You; Seek and You Will Find
Developing Mental Leverage and Hardening Your Will 61
  When The Student Is Ready, The Teacher Will Appear!
The Incredible Power of Visualization 69
  With Our Thoughts We Make Our World
Taking Action Now and Consistently Following Through . . 77
  Courage Has Genius, Power, And Magic In It

References 87

Acknowledgements

As I sit here considering what to write, my mind wanders through my past in search of those people who are most responsible for my being able to complete this book.

The first person who comes to mind and whom I would like to thank is my wife, Aliya, whose love, encouragement, support, and advice greatly aided me in this effort. She is the woman of my dreams, and she inspires me daily to greater and greater heights. Darling, I love you!

I would like to thank our children, Kristina and Nicky, who are constant reminders for me to strive to be the best person I can be and set the best example I can. They continue to teach me invaluable lessons in life. They are both walking their own paths on the way to their individual destinies. They both dream big, and I know they will accomplish big. Never let anyone or anything dilute your dreams. Hold onto them until you make them real. I love you both a great deal!

To My Mother and Father, the two people responsible for me being here, you will always serve as a great inspiration to me. My father, God rest his soul, passed away many years ago and, while he will never hold a physical copy of this book, he has helped me through tough times in many ways, and I know he is very proud of my accomplishments. My Mother has always encouraged me to make the most out of life, and she has supported my many endeavors with heartfelt support. My Mom, my brother, Dan, and my sister, Heather, helped me by reading my initial manuscript and giving me some great input. My Mom and Dan brainstormed the title for the book. Thank you, I love you!

I acknowledge every person I have ever interacted with as I am the sum total of all of my thoughts and actions. I have made myself who I am with every interaction I have had, good or bad, and I am grateful for them all.

Foreward

This is not the first book written on this subject, and I certainly hope that it will not be last. Throughout recorded history people have expressed these same ideas that I repeat in this book albeit in some other language or literary style. I have not discovered a new concept here, although I present it in my own fashion. It is simply my wish to have a positive impact on people's lives by increasing awareness with regard to what each of us is capable of accomplishing. Many times people are exposed to information that simply does not resonate with them, for one reason or another. It is my hope that the way I present the information in this book resonates with you and becomes part of who you are.

There are many other wonderful books and audio programs out there that say, in essence, the same thing that I say here and I encourage you to read and listen to as many as you can. I want you to keep reading and listening to them until you completely believe in your ability to create the life that you may now only dream of. The only thing that is keeping you from realizing your dreams is your delay in beginning the journey. In this book, my intention is to make you aware of the incredible power that lies deep within each of us, to convince you that you can wield this power to your benefit and the benefit of others, and to introduce you to a simple system designed to allow you to focus your thoughts with precision and to link them to your purpose to create the life that you desire and deserve.

Who you have been in the past and who you are now does not control who you can become tomorrow, next month, or next year. The principles and steps outlined in this book will show you how to take your life to the next level.

By diligently applying what's written in this book you will be able to create a life that you once only dreamed was possible. I was a junior high school dropout. I did not even complete the eighth grade. Imagine that. I was a seventh grade graduate, just one year beyond Jethroism. That's a poke at the old TV series, "The Beverly Hillbillies," for those of you who didn't get it.

I'm not sure why, but somehow, at an early age, I allowed myself to totally lose interest in going to school. I had a pretty bad motorcycle wreck early in my seventh year of school that landed me in the University of Virginia Hospital for several weeks with a severe back injury. That was followed by several months of a body cast, which prevented me from sitting up properly. I missed most of that school year and was held back the next year. It was a tough pill to swallow being held back a grade when my interest in school was not that great anyway.

The end result was I quit school, using that as a convenient excuse for my actions. I was young, inexperienced, and not willing to take the advice of my parents or teachers because I thought I had the world pretty much figured out by then. I thought I was doing the right thing at the time because it seemed like the cool thing to do. Don't put much weight in the "cool thing" to do when making major life decisions that will affect you the rest of your life. The cool thing, like any fad, changes frequently based on time and location while the right thing to do remains pretty constant.

Fortunately for me, I quickly learned that I had made a mistake. Unfortunately, it was a mistake that would take literally years to correct. Within months of quitting school I realized my mistake, and it was a big one! I wanted badly to correct it, but I didn't want to go back to junior high school because I was embarrassed. I tried to earn my GED by attending classes at the county's adult basic education program. I went to a few classes and then, for some reason, I'm not even sure why, I was unable to make it happen.

I worked several jobs over the next couple of years, mostly laborer positions that required little education or skills. When I wasn't working I wasted my time sleeping late and hanging out in the local pool hall. I hung out with my friends and partied, after they got out of school.

By the time I was sixteen years old I had firmly recognized that I was totally wasting my life and if I didn't take responsibility and do something about it, I would end up in jail or even worse! Some of my friends had already spent time in jail or were dead as a result of drugs or alcohol-related accidents. That's when I decided to join the army. I was sixteen years old, and my parents were overjoyed at my realization and my decision to join the Army. At that age my mom and dad had to co-sign my contract with the Army. I shipped off for training just after turning seventeen.

The Army gave me something I was unable to give myself at that time, structure and a plan, not to mention three meals a day, a bed, and a regular paycheck. I think I was raking in about $500 per month, before taxes, and since I was stationed overseas in Germany I got an additional $8 per month foreign duty pay.

I didn't know it when I joined, because I hadn't thought that far into the future yet, but I would spend the next 23 years in the Army, retiring in 2003 from the Army's elite Special Forces, or the Green Berets as it's more commonly known. It would take writing another book just to list all the things I did and the lessons I learned, both professionally and personally, while serving in the Green Berets.

I have conducted conventional and special operations all over the world. The men of U.S. Special Operations Command are some of the finest and hardest men in the world. I consider myself lucky to have known and served side-by-side with many of them.

In fact, I would like to take the opportunity here to thank every person who has served in the past, those who continue to serve today, and those who will make the decision to serve in the future. Your sacrifices and those of your families are noted and greatly appreciated.

In early 2004, I became 110% dedicated to discovering what it takes to live life at the highest level possible. That was when I really began to put these principles to the test. I noticed that, when I set a goal, something happens that I don't fully understand and can't clearly explain. It's as if the universe conspires to help me achieve my goals.

You can call it luck, God, Universal Intelligence, or synchronicity but designing and committing to a goal sets in motion a chain of events that are outside of your control—yet you are the initiator and direct beneficiary. Small, unexpected things occur that move you closer to your goals. You have to be acutely aware of what is going on in your life to recognize this passive force. The next time you set a goal, pay close attention and log everything that happens in your life that moves you closer to achieving your goal. Don't just log your actions. Log anything that happens which moves you closer to your goal, whether you actively completed it or it was just a "coincidence." You will notice that, in addition to your intentional actions, these seemingly unplanned coincidences are instrumental and necessary in the achievement of your goal.

To test this, I developed goals that I had no idea how I was going to accomplish at the time I set them. I decided that I wanted to earn at least $20,000 a month in income. Within three months I was earning $27,000 per month. I decided that I wanted to live and work in Dubai. Within months I was living and working in Dubai as a special advisor and trainer to the Rulers of Abu Dhabi and Dubai. It has become like a game for me now. I develop outrageous goals, then go for it just to see if I can manifest them. More often than not, I am able to make them part of my reality.

Since retiring from the Special Forces and beginning to develop and use these principles, I have led anti-terrorist teams in Indonesia for the U.S. Department of State. I was the Team Leader and Deputy Program Manager responsible for developing the Iraqi Bureau of Dignitary Protection, a program developed to train and mentor the bodyguards for the Iraqi Prime Minister, Deputy Prime Minister, President, and two Vice Presidents, as well as 47 other Ministers and Justices.

I have advised and trained members of the royal families in Dubai and Abu Dhabi. I have served as Director for a major British company with global operations, as President of two U.S. companies with global operations, and now I am the Chief Operations Officer for a global security company with offices in multiple countries. I have written this book. I have completed my undergraduate studies, and I'm currently working to complete my graduate studies.

I have taken some incredible vacations with my family, spending one Christmas in Switzerland skiing the Eiger, a New Year's Eve in Paris under the Eiffel Tower, and summer in Saint Petersburg, Russia touring the Hermitage. I have studied yoga and learned to ballroom dance. This list goes on and on, but I think you get the idea.

I have told you a lot about my personal life, my successes as well as some pretty big failures. At first, I was hesitant to write about myself, but I wanted to give you a real life example, up front of someone who started at the bottom with no extraordinary advantages and was able to overcome adversity and create massive success. I got to where I am in life now by deciding to take action. I decided that I was not going to settle for the status quo, that I was going to make life happen for me. So that's what I did through dedicated effort, and applying the principles outlined in this book.

Timothy M. Ferris

If I can do it, you can do it. You and I are the same. I don't care what your race, sex, religion, or socioeconomic status is. We are more alike than we are different, and these principles do not discriminate; they apply to everyone. So, make a promise to yourself right now. Don't wait. Promise that you are not going to sit back any longer and accept whatever comes your way. Instead, you are going to begin to make life happen for you. You are going to design the life of your dreams, and you are going to start taking action now to bring those dreams into reality.

Section 1: Preparing Yourself for Success

WHO ARE YOU NOW AND WHO WILL YOU BE IN THE FUTURE?

IMAGINE THE POSSIBILITIES!

I want to talk about possibility; the possibility that you can make your dreams come true! The possibility that you can design the life you've always dreamed of living and make it happen. I believe that you can live your dreams. And the wonderful thing is, it's not too late. You still believe it, too. If you didn't, you wouldn't be reading this book. Think about that for minute.

What are dreams? Well, in the sense that we are discussing here, dreams are thoughts; thoughts about what we want, what kind of people we would like to be, what kind of things we would like to do, where we would like to live, the kinds of relationships we would like to be in, the kind of work we would like to do, and the list goes on and on.

Everyone at one time or another has dreams. We all have, at some time, dreamed of a better life than we are currently living and experiencing. What happens to most people's dreams? Do you remember what your dreams were when you were a little kid? Do you know what your dreams are now? Have your dreams been glazed over by the mundane routines of everyday life? I'm talking about things like paying your bills, grocery shopping, taking the kids to practice, cleaning the house, and mowing the yard. It's not that these things aren't important. They are, but they are not what most people dream of doing. They are the "implied tasks" of life. All of us have these types of routine tasks that are just part of life. But for some people, these routines have slowly taken a place of importance above their dreams. We can't let that happen!

If you have already allowed your daily routines to eclipse your dreams, then now is the time to change. It's time to wake up to new possibilities and take control of your life instead of passively allowing your life and your external environment to control you. You are in charge. So, you can just sit around passively allowing the external forces of everyday life to push you around, or you can actively take control and become the author of your life by following the steps outlined in this book.

The title of this book, "Mind Energy: The Power of ME!" is meant to communicate a simple truth. We each have total control over our minds and our lives. The mind is the most powerful tool we have. We create our life's situations with every decision we make or fail to make. The message that I want to communicate with "The Power of ME!" is that I (ME), can control and create my life circumstances through my mind's energy by knowing what I want, being decisive, and taking action.

You current situation is a result of your past decisions and actions. A junkie is a junkie, not because someone gave him crack or some other drug, but because he made a decision and took action. A doctor is a doctor, not because her parents sent her to medical school, but because she decided to become a doctor and took the necessary actions to make that her reality.

Make a decision, right now, to be active, not passive! Your future begins now with or without your input. Your future is decided every day, in the now, through your actions, your decisions, and indecisions. Mind Energy refers to power of thought. Thoughts, like the wind, cannot be seen nor touched. But they exist just the same. Through your mind's energy, you create your future in the present with every thought you have and every action you take. Realize this, and you will find great inner strength.

Have your dreams been diluted? You may have allowed yourself to be slowly convinced that your dreams were unreasonable expectations and that you should "come back down to earth." Why would someone sabotage your dreams? Not on purpose. They may be "just trying to keep you from getting hurt" or "giving you the benefit of their life's experience." Do these reasons sound familiar? Realize that they are applying the filters of their life's experience to your life's situation. That is to say, they are using their life's experiences and the lessons, both good and bad, that life has taught them to judge the outcome of your life. Your life is not their life.

You have your own life and your own dreams. Don't let anyone convince you that you can't live the life you want and be the person you know you can be. You owe it to yourself to go out and make life happen for you the way you want it to, on your own terms.

> "With the proper intent, clarity of thought, and effort, anyone is capable of manifesting the life they've always dreamed of." (Tim Ferris, 2008)

Do you know what your dreams are? If you could live life on your own terms, what would your life be like? Take a minute now and think about what your dreams are. Can you see them? Are they vivid with all the color, texture, animation, smells, sights, and sounds of real life? If not, they need to be.

If you can't clearly see the important details of your dreams, then they're just vague thoughts that periodically pop into your mind. Additionally, by not having them defined with laser sharp clarity, they can be different each time you think about them. When this happens, your brain doesn't know what to focus on consistently, so it doesn't look for ways to move you closer to your goals. This is because you have not taken the time to clearly articulate to your mind exactly what your dreams and goals are.

You've allowed them to fade away into the background of your daily life activities.

How does that happen? Well, it doesn't happen all of a sudden. It happens gradually as we allow the people and activities in our life to distract us from our most precious possessions, our life's dreams and the goals we must achieve to reach those dreams. And before we know it, we are stuck in a pattern of behavior where all we care about is the short term; things like waking up and going to a job that we're not thrilled about, what's for dinner, can I pay the bills this month, is my spouse or significant other going to be angry at me for this or that, and any other number of daily recurring routines that don't move us solidly in the direction of our dreams and goals.

A more important question is how can we get back to fulfilling our dreams? Refocusing our mind's eye is the key to getting back on track. There are an incredible number of references, some dating back to antiquity, that tell us what we focus on is what we will experience.

We have control over our minds, or at least we can have control over our minds. That means that we get to make the rules, we get to tell our minds what is important to us, and what is not. Most of us make the small things in life seem most important at the expense of the big things that really matter like relationships, personal development (intellectual, emotional, physical, and spiritual), professional development, and sound financial planning and practices.

Your previous intentions, thoughts, and actions are who you are currently. Your present intentions, thoughts, and actions will determine who you will be in the future. The equation for success in life is simple to understand. It just takes discipline to implement it.

> *Right Intention + Right Thought + Right Action = The Life You Now Dream Of*

Success happens instantly, however, the manifestations of success take time to catch up. There is a necessary lag between one thinking about doing something and actually manifesting that thought into real life. My promise to you is that the tools and strategies I outline in this book will show you how to take control of your life. I will show you how to get back on track by making consistent, incremental changes that will build on one another day after day, leading you to your eventual goals and your chosen destiny. Your promise to you must be that you will follow through by taking the actions necessary to succeed in your goals and your dreams.

The Time To Create Your Future Is Now

Thought Linked to Purpose Becomes Creative Force

Creating the life that you've dreamed of is not impossible, although it may sometimes seem that way to us. The life you want is achievable. Everything is within your grasp once you learn how to focus the incredible power of your thoughts and link them to your chosen purpose.

What do highly successful people know that escapes so many others? Simple: Our mind is the most powerful tool we have. If you can think it, it can be achieved! You just need to be willing to learn and apply some time-tested key concepts. The steps listed below represent a systematic process for achieving your life's dreams. They provide you with an outline, a plan of action, that you can use to shape your future beginning now. I want to emphasize the word "now" here, because now is when your future begins. Achieving your dreams requires an actionable plan and the drive to take action.

—Define Your Life's Purpose by Creating a Life Plan

—Develop Compelling Goals That Support Your Life's Purpose

  —Visualize Your Goals and Dreams; See Them in Your Mind as Already Completed

  —Develop Mental Leverage and Harden Your Will

  —Take Action Starting Now and Follow Through Consistently

The steps I have outlined here represent a proven system for success that I have synthesized from my own experiences. The concepts that I write about in this book are not new. These key concepts have been known and used for millennia. I present them to you here as one path to achieving your goals and your dreams.

There have been many people throughout history who have studied and written about the topic of achievement and what makes people successful. All of these people have done what I am doing here, outlined the system that they used to achieve success. The steps that I use and present to you in this book are not difficult in theory or practice. The main things you are required to possess are a clear vision of what you want, a well thought out plan that includes written goals, a burning desire to achieve it, and focused and consistent action toward the achievement of what you want.

Many people are unaware that there is a system of thinking, which if adapted, allows us to tap into an unseen force. It allows us to use our mind's energy with greater precision, and in turn, results in the manifestation of those thoughts that we habitually focus on, whether they be good or bad.

If someone showed you the skills necessary to achieve your goals and make your dreams come true, would you use them? If you had a User's Manual for your brain, would you read it?

When purchasing a new computer it contains a User's Manual that explains exactly how to use that computer to its maximum potential. How many people actually read that manual and how many of people just turn on the computer and start using it, learning to use it in a haphazard trial and error fashion? The really successful people out there spend the time and energy required to learn how to get the most out of the resources they have at hand and get the most our of everything they choose to do.

We did not get a User's Manual with our minds. For most of us, we were not directly taught what I consider to be among the most basic and important life skills necessary to be able to take full advantage of the incredible power of our minds, which will allow us to live life to its fullest. Many people do go on to discover this knowledge on their own, but for most of us that discovery is in the haphazard form of trial and error mentioned earlier, which often takes a great deal of time, causing the realization to occur later in life. There is a better way, a more effective and more efficient way.

Role modeling is a much more effective and efficient path to success than the old trial and error process. You can learn from others' experiences and use their models for success. You have the rest of your life to learn from your trials and errors. Why not give yourself a head start on success by observing and learning from others who have been there and done that? Most highly successful people who are in touch with their life's purpose are keenly aware of the methods that work for them and the methods that do not.

It is commonplace for people to make incorrect assumptions about the successes of others. One common reaction is to assume, "that person is so lucky" or "that person was born into a successful set of circumstances and handed the proverbial silver spoon." Yes, there are some people who are born into their circumstances, but highly successful people who continue to be high achievers are not just lucky. They worked hard to get to their current level of achievement in life, and they continue to work hard to remain at that level. They also followed a set of principles designed to optimize their chances of success.

When you look at people like Bill Gates (founder of Microsoft), Serge Brin and Larry Page (founders of Google), Arnold Schwarzenegger (body builder, actor, governor), Michael Jordan (professional basketball player), or Warren Buffet (investor, businessman, and philanthropist) you need to know with certainty that they were not just lucky nor born under the right star. They developed a plan, set goals, worked hard, and made calculated risks to get where they are today. You can bet that they didn't just stumble into success and that they have a success system that they use to achieve their goals and dreams.

What are you truly capable of accomplishing by linking thought to purpose? Let's consider some of the truly amazing examples of what people have accomplished in recent history that clearly demonstrates the awesome power of what we, humans, are capable of when our thoughts are linked to a compelling purpose. We have put people in space and on the moon with the power of our minds.

We have explored the outer reaches of our solar system with the Voyager I and II programs. We have landed spacecraft on Mars and explored its geology and atmosphere while controlling everything remotely from Earth. We have explored the depths of the oceans. We have developed computers and computer networks that allow us to transmit data and communicate instantly across great distances. We can now type a word or phrase into a search engine like Google and instantly retrieve more usable information on that topic than you could read in a lifetime. We have identified some of the world's most deadly and debilitating diseases, discovered cures for them, and in some cases totally eradicated them for our world.

We have taken what was once science fiction, someone's thoughts, and by linking it to purpose, intention, and direction we have made new realities. All of the achievements I mentioned above began as thoughts by people just like you and me. Any one of these achievements should be inspiration and evidence enough for us to know that dreams really do come true, if we take the necessary steps to make them come true.

Now, what is your answer to the question, can you make your dreams come true? My answer to that question is a simple and resounding, "Yes!" You can create the life you desire through designing a purpose for your life, a life plan used to guide you on your journey to your ultimate destiny, creating clear mental images of yourself living your chosen life's purpose, deciding that you can and will take action, systematically setting goals that are supportive of and aligned with your vision and again using your powers of visualization to see your goals attained, and last, disciplining yourself to consistently take action that moves you in the direction of your goals and dreams. By using your mind in a disciplined and deliberate manner you can move closer to your goals and dreams each day. Simply link thought to purpose, to focus the power of your thoughts on achieving your life's purpose and mentally prod yourself to take action

I would like to share with you one of my favorite quotes from an incredibly gifted and insightful man who lived over a century ago. This quote speaks about the incredible power within each us. All we have to do is learn how to harness it and how to use it to fuel us on the journey to our chosen destiny. James Allen was an English poet and philosopher who spent his last nine years writing books that outlined his deep understanding of the human condition and how to improve it. In his most well known literary work, <u>As A Man Thinketh</u>, he wrote this:

> *"Man is made or unmade by himself; in the armory of thought he forges the weapons by which he destroys himself; he also fashions the tools with which he builds for himself heavenly mansions of joy and strength and peace. By the right choice and true application of thought, man ascends to the Divine Perfection; by the abuse and wrong application of*

thought, he descends below the level of the beast. Between these two extremes are all the grades of character, and man is their maker and master.

Of all the beautiful truths pertaining to the soul which have been restored and brought to light in this age, none is more gladdening or fruitful of divine promise and confidence than this – that man is the master of thought, the molder of character, and the maker and shaper of condition, environment, and destiny.

A man is literally what he thinks, his character being the complete sum of all of his thoughts."(James Allen, 1902).

In this quote, James Allen tells us that we are the makers of ourselves through our thoughts. We create our circumstances, good and bad, by the thoughts that we harbor and dwell on in our minds.

The principle that he wrote about in this quote is not some obscure secret. In the past there have been many people who were aware of and applied these principles as evidenced by the writings they, or people who knew them, left for us. Some of the more well known people who possessed this knowledge were Jesus Christ, the Buddha, Marcus Aurelius, Michelangelo, Leonardo Da Vinci, Ralph Waldo Emerson, and Henry David Thoreau, and that's just to name a few.

An impressive number of scholars, philosophers, holy men, kings, emperors, and yes, ordinary guys like me have learned these principles and used them to create a better life. There are also many contemporary writers and speakers who have made it their life's work to educate people on these principles so that those people might realize their true potential, improve their life's situation, and feel the passion and enjoyment that every person has the right to experience in their daily life.

You can create the life that you dream of by following these simple steps:

- Decide what your life's purpose is going to be and develop a life plan that supports it.
- Design a set of specific and compelling goals that are aligned with and support your life's purpose.
- Develop mental leverage on yourself and harden your will.
- Visualize yourself succeeding by creating a vivid mental image of yourself living your life's purpose and accomplishing your goals.
- The next step is to take action and consistently follow through.

In Part II of this book, I have devoted a chapter to each of these steps so that each can be discussed in detail, and I have included a practical exercise at the end of each of those chapters that will guide you through each of the steps. Be sure to do these practical exercises. If you truly want positive change, it's all about taking action.

You are the observer, the life force that animates your physical body, and you have the power to control your internal world, your mind and thoughts. That's where everything begins. Thoughts that you focus your attention on over long periods of time tend to manifest themselves in your external world. It doesn't matter if they are good thoughts or bad thoughts. What you focus on in your internal world, your mind, you tend to manifest into your external world, your physical life.

It's important to control your thoughts and not allow your thoughts to control you. You must constantly guard against negative, unwanted thoughts, weeding them out of your mind and replacing them with positive, empowering ones. Don't accept this just because I say it's so. Read this book and apply these principles in earnest, and you will find that what is written here actually works. There is no down side to giving this a try. At the very least, you will learn more about yourself and what you truly want in life. At the very most, you will discover a truth that has been known and practiced for thousands of years, a truth that can help you make your dreams come true if you apply it.

There is no shortage of people who believed in this principle, applied it to their own lives, and taught it to others. Jesus Christ said, "As you think, so shall it be." Aristotle said, "The energy of the mind is the essence of life." And Marcus Aurelius said, "Such as are your habitual thoughts, such also will be the character of your mind; for the soul is dyed by the thoughts."

These people speak to us through their writings from ages long past. They lived in different times and in different worlds, culturally and socially speaking. But the principles behind what they believed are still just as valid today as they were during their lives so many years ago. They are truths that do not change with time.

Throughout this book I use quotes from famous people to highlight many of the points I want to drive home. I want to close this chapter by offering you a brilliant quote from a brilliant man, Leonardo da Vinci.

> *"It had long since come to my attention that people of accomplishment rarely sat back and let things happen to them. They went out and happened to things." Leonardo da Vinci (1452-1519)*

This quote by a man who is still considered to be one of the greatest minds that ever lived is one of my favorite quotes of all time. Take heed of this quote and resolve today that you are no longer going to just sit back and let things happen to you. Rather, you are going to happen to things. Beginning now, resolve that you are going to happen to things in such a way that you begin to manifest your goals and your dreams!

Understanding the Silent Killer of Success:

Simple Methods for Recognizing and Breaking Through Procrastination

In the previous chapters, my goal was to make you aware of the amazing possibilities that exist for anyone who has the faith and courage to go out in life and create opportunities instead of simply accepting whatever comes along. I introduced you to a five-step process which can be followed to begin creating a powerful future.

In this chapter, I want to discuss what is quite possibly the single biggest killer of success in achieving your goals and dreams, procrastination. I want to arm you with this information up front so that you are aware of it and how to avoid its destructive patterns that threaten to derail your efforts before you even begin them.

What is Procrastination? The definition according to Merriam-Webster's Collegiate Dictionary is: "To put off intentionally and habitually: to put off intentionally the doing of something that should be done."

Procrastination has been called the silent killer of dreams and the death rattle to success. In simple terms, when you procrastinate, you are sabotaging your future. You are neglecting to do things that could have a profound positive impact on the professional, personal, emotional, financial, and relational areas of your life, your ultimate destiny!

We create our destiny every day with the decisions we make, or fail to make. So why not learn how to use our minds to overcome behaviors that shut down our ability to act in a way that will take us in a more positive direction. To succeed, we need to act in such a way that our decisions and our actions will take us in the direction of success.

Who can be affected by procrastination? Everyone. There is no discrimination when it comes to this undesirable character trait. Everyone is affected by procrastination at some point. It affects men and women, young and old, people with little responsibility and accountability to people with great responsibility and accountability.

For someone who habitually procrastinates, it generally affects all areas of their life; putting off doing income taxes, waiting until it's too late to get that gift or card for someone special, putting off doing work or school projects until the last possible minute, and the list goes on and on. By now, you should have a pretty good image of someone like this in your mind, maybe someone who is close to you like a family member, a friend, or a work colleague, or maybe even yourself!

So what's the difference between someone who is proactive and productive and someone who is not? People who are proactive and productive have learned to recognize that they have specific behavioral patterns that lead to procrastination. As soon as they start to run one of those patterns, they habitually and intentionally interrupt it by taking action and doing what needs to be done. They simply put off procrastination.

If you know you are a procrastinator and you know you are good at it, you should use it to your advantage, right? You should have no problems just putting it off. Procrastinate on procrastinating until you finish that which needs to be done. Once you're finished, then you can procrastinate. Actually, instead of calling it procrastination, at this point let's call it relaxing after a job well done.

What is the basic psychology behind procrastination? People generally procrastinate to avoid the pain they associate with just doing the task in question. In short, people who habitually procrastinate do so because they want to avoid perceived difficulty and focus on the perceived pleasure they will experience in the near-term by opting to avoid that which needs to be done, often preferring to watch TV, talk on the phone, eat, clean their desk, as well as many other behavior patterns. They are in a manner of speaking addicted to the feeling of these near-term pleasures. This avoidance is at the expense of their future.

People who are proactive have learned how to by-pass near-term pleasures in exchange for what they know will ultimately lead to a greater pleasure; a sense of accomplishment and fulfillment. Proactive people become addicted to the experience of achievement, knowing that the sooner they accomplish that which needs to be done, the sooner they will experience the much greater pleasure of achievement and moving closer to their dreams.

It has been suggested that as much as 70% of the population experience negative affects in their lives because they procrastinate. I believe that the percentage is even higher. The point is that there are a lot of people who allow their behavior, procrastination, to keep them from realizing their full potential and living the life that they dream of and deserve.

What are the effects of procrastination? By procrastinating you are putting off doing something that needs to be done. Deep down inside you know it needs to be done. This can cause you to experience some strong, negative emotions; inadequacy, guilt, depression, fear, etc. In addition, your actions can lead to those closest to you experiencing the pain of negative emotions. People who are counting on you to accomplish certain things will process your actions, or lack thereof, in a negative way. By putting off things that they are counting on you to do, you are not fulfilling your responsibilities to them and, in the process you are not only letting yourself down, you are letting them down, too.

The negative effects of this can be quite significant for businesses as well. Procrastination can shut down creativity and productivity, affecting the corporate culture. Employers pay a heavy price in the form of low work output and low quality work. The reduced output is because of habitual patterns of constantly putting off things that need to be done.

Time stops for no one, and deadlines will continue to get closer and closer until eventually your brain will decide that the consequences of not doing it will ultimately be more painful than just doing it. Once you reach that point, your focus will shift, and you will start to work at a frenzied pace to get it done by the deadline.

It's like when you were in school and you had an assignment that you didn't want to do. You would think about doing it, and all of the images in your head would be about how difficult it would be and how much work you would have to do or how you would rather be doing something else, anything but your assignment. Then at some point, maybe one or two days before it was due, your brain would realize that if you didn't start now and finish it, you would experience pain; the pain of an "F" or an incomplete grade. That's the point when your brain would switch sides and you would focus on getting it done to avoid the pain of an "F". The problem with this pattern is that your work is usually of a much lower quality than what you are actually capable of producing.

I remember walking into an office one time and seeing a sign that read, "If you wait until the last minute to do something, it only takes a minute to get it done." If you are one of the people who believe this, then I suggest you rethink that. The negative effects of procrastination always affect the bottom line. For businesses and individuals it means less success.

To combat procrastination we need to understand some of the basic psychology of behind it. We already said previously that someone who procrastinates is avoiding the perceived difficulty and pain of a task, opting instead for a more comfortable and pleasurable behavior. What are some examples of situations that would trigger this behavior? There are a multitude of reasons why people procrastinate. As you consider these examples, remember that the essence of procrastination is putting something off intentionally and habitually.

Some people may feel that they lack the skills to get the job done properly. They would prefer to have people think that they lack the effort or motivation rather than lacking the skill to get it done, saying, "I can do it if I want to. I just don't feel like doing it now."

It could be a time management problem and a failure to prioritize tasks. People may make poor distinctions between what is actually important and what may seem important due to its proximity or urgency. For example, maintaining your car is important. It's something that has to be done to ensure safe and reliable transportation. It should be scheduled and done before something breaks. Once something breaks it requires urgent attention, many times at the expense of other important things. Why not plan ahead and take care of things before they become urgent?

Some people may have poorly developed decision-making skills. One pattern for people who have poor decision-making skills is to simply put off making an important decision, maybe due to uncertainty about the outcome of a particular course of action or fear of accepting responsibility for the decision. I call this "analysis paralysis." These people are paralyzed as a result of overanalyzing the situation or possibly because of the sheer scope of the decision.

When a need for action is first identified, there are generally multiple courses of action available, and they are all time sensitive. As time keeps ticking away, the options available keep falling by the wayside until eventually time leaves only one option. People who have fallen into this pattern of behavior have effectively put off making the decision themselves and allowed time to make it for them. One could rationalize that he/she did not make the decision and should not bear responsibility for it. However, that is not true. Their decision to be indecisive is what actually led to the final course of action.

Some people fear failure. Believe it or not, there are also people who fear success. It's easy to understand how someone could fear failure, but how could someone be afraid of success? Well, in their mind they associate success with images that are bad, as opposed to images that are good. They focus on the things that they perceive as the negative outcomes associated with success. They make these negative images seem so intense that success would feel like a burden to them.

How could this be? They focus on how success could lead to a promotion, which is a positive thing, yet that would lead additional unwanted responsibility, and that would be a negative thing. A promotion would mean making more money, and that would mean having to pay more taxes. Who wants to pay more taxes? It would also mean more effort to manage it. They may have to move to a new group of peers as a result of a promotion or change of job position. That would mean leaving their old friends behind.

Some people are perfectionists and have unrealistic beliefs that a task has to be done a specific way and to a specific standard. It's great to set high standards for yourself as long as they are realistic.

Personally, I focus on workable solutions. I would rather have the 95% solution to a problem and implement it in a timely fashion than wait for the ever-elusive 100% solution. In many cases you can implement a totally acceptable solution, and then improve on it after implementation. This allows you to begin your work, get your ideas out there sooner, and not get bogged down trying to achieve an unreasonable or unattainable result. Get the ball rolling and begin to create momentum. This principle is paramount for companies to retain a competitive edge in today's global business environment.

Some people are overwhelmed because the task is too complicated or large. In some cases a task may be overwhelmingly large and complex, and in other cases you could be making the proverbial "mountain out of the mole hill" by simply perceiving the task as too large or complicated. In either case, remember this, everything can be broken down, grouped together, manipulated, or reframed in some fashion to make it more easily understood or more acceptable to our minds. You don't have to be able to create Gantt charts or conduct a critical path analysis. Simply learn how to reframe complex problems in your mind by breaking them down and developing solutions with more easily manageable steps.

As you can see, the causes of procrastination are many and it is a complex subject. Whatever your reason(s) for procrastination, you are cheating yourself out of the enjoyment and personal growth that comes from meeting a challenge head-on, overcoming the inevitable obstacles, and finally succeeding in producing the results that you want. By simply learning to recognize and interrupt procrastination, you will experience a tremendous boost in the quality of every aspect of your of life; personal, professional, emotional, financial, and relational.

How can you recognize patterns of procrastination in yourself and others? Procrastination is a behavioral pattern. Remember the definition? It is intentionally and habitually putting off that which should be done. Each of us has our own specific behavioral patterns that lead to procrastination. The key is to be able to recognize when you are about to procrastinate so that you can begin to interrupt that pattern as early as possible. By interrupting it, I mean switching from that behavioral pattern to one that allows you to get on with the task at hand.

With enough practice you will have inculcated new behaviors designed to interrupt procrastination automatically. You will have installed a new and empowering behavioral pattern, one that promotes taking action now.

Here are some examples of behavioral patterns indicative of procrastination. These are common things that people do to avoid doing a more challenging, complex, or important task:

- Doing tasks that are routine and unimportant at the expense of other more important tasks.
- Repetitiveness, such as unnecessarily checking your email many times a day or even many times an hour.
- Doing mindless tasks like continuously cleaning and organizing your desk, watching too much television, surfing the Internet with no specific purpose, day dreaming, etc.
- Beginning to work on an important task, not being able to focus, then redirecting your efforts to something different and less important because the scope of the task seems overwhelming.

You can see that all of these patterns lead to one thing; putting off a task that is important, a task that you know you need to do. Instead of meeting the challenge head on you decide to focus your efforts on less important tasks that you are more comfortable with or that are more fun in the immediate moment. Don't do that!

What can you do to break through your patterns of procrastination?

I want you to focus on two words from the definition of procrastination, intentionally and habitually. So far we have clearly defined procrastination, learned of the effects of procrastination, taken a quick look at the basic psychology of procrastination, and discovered how to recognize patterns of procrastination in ourselves and others. Now let's learn how to break through our patterns of procrastination so that we can get the job done and live the quality life that we deserve.

A key step in breaking through procrastination is to know why you procrastinate in the first place. Self-honesty is important here. If you procrastinate simply because you lack the motivation to get on with the job, you need to come up with ways to spur yourself into action. If you are missing deadlines because you lack good organizational skills, you can quickly overcome the problem by learning some solid time management and organizational skills that will help you get organized, prioritize, and get started. Here are some things you can do to break through procrastination and develop empowering behavioral patterns.

Plan your day and review your top goals. Spend some time each morning or the evening prior to plan your day. Don't let life push you around. Take control of your activities and make life happen for you. By spending a small amount of time planning your day and reviewing your goals, your mind will be focused on what really needs to get accomplished, based on what's important to you now, and it will look for opportunities to get it done. You will be amazed at how much more you can accomplish by developing this simple habit.

Make a to-do-list of prioritized tasks. Make a list of the important tasks that you need to accomplish. Prioritize the list from most important to least important. Start with the most important task on your list. If a task seems too big and overwhelming, chunk it down into smaller tasks with more easily manageable steps. By chunking it down into simpler steps you will feel less overwhelmed by it.

Mark off completed tasks. When you complete a task, scratch it off your list. It's funny, but few things feel better than scratching a line through completed tasks on our to-do-lists. Am I right? It is an acknowledgement that we are accomplishing those things that are most important to us.

We do not always get to choose our tasks since our parents, teachers, spouses, and bosses also request that we do things. You may say, "It's not my task. It's a task my boss, teacher, or parent wants me to complete. It's not important to me; it's important to them." Listen, a task should be at least as important to you as the person is who asked you to do the task. So if your job is important to you and your boss asks you to do something, then that makes your boss is important to you, right? If graduating high school or college is important to you and your teacher or professor asks you to do a project, then your teacher and that project are important to you. Learn to look beyond the immediate connections to a task and see how it can impact on your life in the future.

Once the first task is taken care of, it's time to move on to the next one. Since we never run out of things to do in our lives, we must continuously update our physical or mental to-do-lists. Tasks must be periodically reevaluated and adjusted to reflect their level of importance. Life is about change and growth. As we change and grow, our beliefs are altered and our priorities change. That means things that once weren't important may be important now.

By following these simple suggestions, you will make considerable progress in eliminating a destructive behavioral pattern and the killer of your success. This is by no means an exhaustive list of ways to avoid procrastinating. After reading this chapter, I know you will not procrastinate in looking for more ways to kick your life into high gear and start living life at a higher level.

The Past Does Not Equal The Future

Who You Are Today Does Not Control Who You Can Become

I have had some pretty tough challenges in my life. I don't want to make this into an autobiography, but I do want to highlight my point that no matter your circumstances and life situation today, you can change everything beginning now. Some people go from bad situations to great situations, but beware, this is a two-way street, and it can go the other direction too. Every day there are news reports about highly accomplished people, often a celebrity, who had the world by the tail and, through the wrong application of him/herself, let it all fall apart.

Life in the real world is kind of like the stock market. You've probably read or heard the disclaimer statement, "Past returns are not an indication of future performance." That's just as true for your life as it is for investing. What you have accomplished (or failed to accomplish) in the past has no bearing on what you can accomplish (or fail to accomplish) in the future.

Take me. I consider myself to be an accomplished person in life at this point, and I intend to continue to push myself to new heights, growing more and more with each new challenge.

However, I wasn't always like this. I was pretty troubled as a young child. I'm sure I was a tremendous challenge for my parents. I believe people are responsible for their actions beginning at a young age, and I take full responsibility for all of my decisions going back to when I was quite young, five or six years old. In short, I developed a dislike for school and by the time I was fourteen years old, I had quit school. I didn't even finish the eighth grade!

Now, you would think, and rightly so, that a person who only finished the seven years of primary education was destined for a life of . . . well, let's say less than inspiring accomplishment. That has not been the case with me. I have filled my life with extraordinary accomplishments because I know that I can do anything I set my mind to. Academically, I completed my high school studies in the army and earned my GED, I have earned an Associate's degree in foreign language, I have earned a Bachelor's degree in liberal arts, I am halfway through an Executive Master of Business Administration program at the University of Texas at Dallas, and I intend to earn a PhD. So you can see that a person's past has nothing to do with his/her possible future.

In my own life, I can look back and identify times where the success principles discussed in this book were at work. I did not know nor did I recognize it at the time, but in retrospect I do. I'm sure, as you think about your past, you, too, can come up with times when these principles were at work in your life, but you were unaware of it at the time. I'm talking about times when you felt as though everything was right on track and you were unstoppable in achieving your goals, times when you had the feeling that all the right pieces were falling into all the right places. The key to living the life you dream of is to learn these principles and put them to work consistently in all areas of your life.

Before I was fully aware of these principles and how to use them to my advantage, my successes were sporadic and infrequent. I pursued my individual goals without a solid plan for achieving them, and my goals were not linked to my life's purpose. In fact,

I wasn't even aware of what my life's purpose was back then. At that time, I had not yet defined my life's purpose. I did not have a clearly developed life plan outlining what I wanted to accomplish in life, what I wanted my life to mean each and every day. I only had a feeling deep inside that something was missing and that my life was meant to be much more.

For example, I decided to buy a car, so I focused my attention on that desire and did what I needed to do to make that happen. I dealt with each step along the way as I was confronted with each one, and ultimately I achieved my goal. In short, I was driven mostly by impulse, and my goals were developed in a somewhat isolated fashion as single events without consideration for how they may impact on me later in life. I did not take the time to think through what I was doing and if it was the best decision to support my overall life plan, because at the time I did not have an overall life plan. I just did it and reacted to the cascade of events that followed instead of being in control of the situation from the beginning.

With a well thought-out life plan, I could have considered how the car I wanted to purchase and all of the responsibilities and additional expenses that went along with that purchase were going to impact all other areas of my life in the future. By not considering that, I was operating in a reactionary mode. The problem with going for it without a plan was that I was inadequately prepared for the consequences and the inevitable decision points that I was confronted with in the aftermath of my actions.

This is just one simple example that works well to illustrate my point because virtually everyone will face this situation. It is a major life purchase for most people and like all major decision points, it is something that warrants some thought as to how it *will* impact on other areas of your life. My point is for you to take control of your life. Don't leave it up to a car salesman to tell you how much you can afford to pay every month. You may want a BMW and you may be able to qualify for and acquire a BMW, but that doesn't mean that a BMW is the best choice for you when you consider how that purchase will impact all the other areas of your life in the future.

A well thought-out goal allows me to consider, in advance, if my actions support my life plan and how events will unfold to proactively develop actions designed to keep my goal on track. It also allows me to emplace control measures designed to guide me from one decision point to the next. I also use control measures to alert me when I may be exposing myself to more risk than I'm comfortable with. We'll talk more about developing POWERFUL goals in Chapter 2.2 as well as do some useful practical exercises in goal development.

Having a well-defined life plan that details what's important in your life is the surest way to avoid bad situations that can come from making decisions in a reactionary mode. Knowing what's important to you and having a life plan will greatly assist you in making decisions, big and small. It will allow you to identify opportunities and take actions that support your life plan and avoid those that do not. Many people find themselves in undesirable circumstances because they acted without taking the time to consider the cascade of events, good and bad, which will ultimately stem from their decisions and actions. That's how people find themselves with more debt than they can handle. It's how people find themselves in relationships, personal and professional, that may be more one sided than not.

I am going to use a simple metaphor here to more clearly illustrate the positive benefits that result from creating a life plan based on a compelling life's purpose supported by a clear set of well-defined and integrated goals linked to that purpose. This metaphor is about finding your way in a wilderness and the importance of knowing how to correctly use a map and compass to get from one point on the ground to another. The wilderness represents life, and the map and compass are tools that represent having a life's purpose and supportive goals.

Before I learned and applied the principles outlined in this book, moving through my life felt as if I was trying to navigate through a wilderness without a map and a compass. I had not taken the time to assess my current life situation, so I had not accurately identified my current location [life situation] and I did not have a well thought-out and planned destination [a life purpose/life plan]. I was missing the most basic ingredients necessary to get from point A [my current location] to point B [my desired location].

To navigate from point A to point B, you must begin with certain basic information, which includes your current position [life situation], and your desired destination [in life this represents your dreams, your ultimate destiny].

Life with its infinite possibilities is the environment that you must navigate through. To do this, you must also possess certain tools designed to help you find your way and you must know how to use them. First, you need a map that depicts the terrain you must traverse [in life this is the mental image you have developed in your mind of who you want to be, which gives you a visual indication of the path you need to take]. Second, you need a compass to accurately determine your direction and keep you on bearing during the many legs of your journey [in life your compass is represented by the goals and milestones you need to achieve to live your life's purpose and reach your desired destiny, which is the life you now only dream of].

I wandered through life aimless in many important areas of my life because I had not yet made these distinctions and did not possess the tools and strategies I needed to plan and move my life to the next level. My situation felt as though I was moving through a dense forest with lots of undergrowth that obstructed my long-range view. I had not taken the time to accurately define my current life situation, so I was missing an accurately defined starting point [point A]. I had not yet chosen my life's purpose and developed a life plan, so I did not have a clearly defined destination [point B]. Without a clearly defined destination there's not much need for a compass [supportive goals that lead you to your destination].

As I moved through this difficult and often confusing terrain called life, I encountered many obstacles. Some were insurmountable with my then limited knowledge, skills, and abilities. Many would change my course because I lacked the necessary strategies and tools to overcome them, which necessarily caused me to take the path of least resistance. I was channeled into taking the easy way out, which didn't always give me the result I wanted. Had I known then what I know now and applied it, I would have conquered many of those early obstacles, and I would have enjoyed a much greater quality of life than I did. I would have been better equipped to make the most out of life if I had created a life plan and designed powerful goals to support that plan.

As it was, occasionally I would come upon a clearing [an isolated goal, a moment of clarity, where I knew what I wanted if only in the short term] in the middle of this dark forest. From the forest's edge I would be able to see to the far side of the clearing where the forest began again. On the far side I could see a goal that I wanted to reach, and I would use that to set my bearing. In this example, the goal I'm speaking of represents one of my short-term, isolated goals like buying a car, buying a house, or getting a promotion, finding someone to spend the rest of my life with, etc. Standing on the edge of a clearing, I could see exactly where I needed to go on the other side to reach that goal.

Of particular note is that I had not even considered how achieving this goal would impact the rest of my journey. Once I had achieved it, I was back in the forest with no direction or bearing for where I wanted to go next, so again I would wander through my life without a clear long-term purpose or direction. I did not have a well-defined life's purpose, a life plan, to serve as an internal compass to provide direction that would guide me through life when things got fuzzy and confusing. So, I would continue to wander through life until I came upon another clearing, another isolated, short-term goal. I would pursue that goal, then I would be back in the dark wandering around again.

That's pretty much how my life went until I learned and began to use these simple principles.

Wandering through life without any form of a plan and being buffeted around by external forces is not the path to an incredible and fulfilling life. That's no way for you to live life, when you can live an extraordinary life filled with purpose, direction, and a passion.

Life at that level is not really living, but merely existing at a basic level by meeting some or all of your basic needs. It is certainly not what Abraham Maslow had in mind when he wrote about self-actualization in his Theory of Human Motivation where he wrote, "the desire for self-fulfillment, namely the tendency for him [the individual] to become actualized in what he is potentially. This tendency might be phrased as the desire to become more and more what one is, to become everything that one is capable of becoming." (Maslow, 1943)

One of the most enlightening and exhilarating possibilities that I can contemplate is realizing that people can take immediate control of their life and begin to change their circumstances, in essence becoming the author of their life by creating their future with their present thoughts and actions.

Your future is the sum total of the thoughts and actions you have in the present. The only way to affect your future is by taking action now, in the present. I have already said that to go from one location on the ground to another, you must first know where you are, second where you are going, and third, know how to get there, or the best path for you to take. The same is true of your life. To change your life situation, you must first know where you are, second, you must know where you want to be, and third, you must have a plan to get from where you are to where you want to be, the path you want to take to close the gap. Designing an overarching purpose for your life, a life plan, gives your mind vital information about what's important to you. It tells your mind the direction that you want your life to move in.

Some people go through life achieving goal after goal and even making incredible progress only to find out later that they are totally unfulfilled because their life's overall direction was wrong. Yes, they made significant progress, but they were traveling in a direction that was wrong for them, and the ultimate destination left them feeling empty and disappointed.

Some people focus all of their attention on one area of life, like a relationship or work, neglecting the other important areas in their life and failing to maintain the necessary balance that leads to a well rounded and completely fulfilling life experience. There are many who achieved fame and greatness in one area of their life and allowed it all to fall apart by neglecting other areas, or worse, died as a result of suicide or overdose because they were totally unhappy even though they were highly successful in one area.

I achieved most of those isolated goals I set, and I felt a great sense of pride, accomplishment, and fulfillment at the time I achieved them, but those emotions were short lived. There was still something missing in my life. Even after achieving what I considered major accomplishments there was something missing in the time intervals between those accomplishments.

It was like a roller coaster ride with ups, when I was working to achieve my goals and at the moments of my achievements, and downs, when I wasn't actively working toward a goal. There was a lack of consistency in my emotional experiences. I wanted to feel that sense of accomplishment and fulfillment that you experience when you accomplish something, big or small, on a more consistent basis. I wanted balance in my life.

By deciding on an overarching purpose for your life, you can experience a sense of pride, accomplishment, and fulfillment everyday if you like. How can you do that? By knowing that every day you are living your life's purpose that you designed in your life plan. Your life plan is a yardstick that you can use to measure your success. How can you measure your success if you don't have a basis for the measurement?

Since I had not yet chosen and developed my life's purpose back then, I did not experience high levels of emotions like accomplishment and fulfillment on a consistent basis. I only experienced them when I was working toward and accomplishing a short-term goal.

Now, I experience a sense of pride, accomplishment, and fulfillment every single day. Why? Because I have a plan that supports my life's purpose and is my map to life. I can use it to measure my progress along the journey to make sure I'm on track and making what I consider to be satisfactory progress toward that end.

In the past, I was motivated to make the most out of life. I just didn't know what to do because I didn't have a clearly defined life's purpose with a supporting life plan. That is where the frustration and the feeling of something lacking in my life came from. I knew I wanted more, but I had not taken the time to clearly indentify what I wanted. Additionally, back then I did not possess the necessary skills and knowledge to make it happen. I was unaware of a success system, like the tools and strategies I'm presenting to you in this book, which enable one to take full advantage of life's unlimited opportunities and create a powerful future.

If you are completely satisfied in all areas of your life because you are living your dreams now, I commend you. You are one of the few who has discovered the keys to your personal success. I recommend that you keep doing what you are currently doing and continue to build and improve on your successes by seeking new tools and strategies outside of your personal system. You can always learn something by going outside your system and studying other systems.

On the other hand, if you are motivated to make your dreams come true, but feel frustrated because your progress is not at the level you would like, this book is definitely for you. Take the mental tools and strategies in this book and put them to work. Develop your life's purpose and create a life plan that includes a set of goals aligned with your life's purpose.

You are taking the first step by reading this book. Create momentum in your life by disciplining yourself to take consistent action every day that moves you in the direction of your goals and dreams. Don't be discouraged when it takes longer than expected. Be happy that every day you are making progress in the direction of your goals and dreams even if the progress is small. As I mentioned earlier, some of my goals have literally taken years, but I never lost sight of them, and I never lost faith in my ability to manifest them. Some took longer because I put them on the backburner when my priorities changed, and I resumed them at a later point when the time was right for me. So, the point I want to drive home is this. Do not get discouraged, keep faith, and keep taking small, incremental steps toward your goals and dreams.

Section 2: Creating a Compelling Future Step-By-Step

Defining Your Life's Purpose and Creating a Life Plan

Discovering What's Important To You

Now that you've read through the first section you should be pretty motivated to take your life to the next level. The first step in the process is to figure out what your purpose is. How do we know what our life's purpose is? Do we wait for an epiphany or some prompt that originates outside of us? Do we just keep living and doing things the way we have always done until one of these things occurs and all of a sudden we know what our purpose is? The question, "Why am I here?" has challenged mankind since its origin.

I want to offer you one answer to the question, "Why am I here?" and "What is the meaning of my life?" speaking on an individual level as opposed to why we, mankind, are here. The answer is simple. Each of us gets to choose what we want our lives to mean. You get to choose what the purpose of your life is. The decision is literally yours to make.

When I first learned that you get to choose a purpose for your life I was listening to Get The Edge, a Tony Robbins audio program. He explained how each person gets to design their life's purpose. Wow! I had never thought of it quite like that. We don't have to wait for some lofty purpose to come to us. We can design our own life's purpose statement based on what we want to be important to us. We can base it on what is important to us or what we want to be important to us from this point on. We get to "set the game up for success," as he put it.

At the time, I was driving across the Arabian desert in my Jaguar. Okay, it was really my wife's Jaguar. I remember pulling off the road and resolving not to move until I had developed "My Life's Purpose Statement" at least in a draft form. And that's exactly what I did. I sat there in the scorching desert heat surrounded by endless sand dunes with mirages rising off the road and the temperature hitting somewhere around 120+ degrees Fahrenheit, although, with my A/C set at a comfortable 70 degrees.

I carefully considered what I wanted to be important to me. I didn't focus only on what was important to me at the time because what was important to me at the time was obviously not causing me to feel the feelings that I wanted to experience on a daily basis. I evaluated everything important to me and considered what else I wanted to be important to me to experience the feelings I wanted, which was more passion and excitement, and better balance and consistency in my experiences in all areas of my life. This is what I came up with that day:

> "I will be a loving, caring and understanding husband / father / friend / person who learns and grows every day so that I can contribute back to the cycle of knowledge by teaching others in an informative and entertaining way that creates the tides of positive change and makes a lasting impact on our lives!"

This was my new mission, my newly drafted life's purpose, and although I have expanded it and some of the wording has changed, it is still a valid part of my life's purpose today. This simple statement serves as my internal compass and I use it to keep my life on track and get back on track when I get confused and feel as though I am losing my way. It also serves as the yardstick that I use to measure my progress. Each day I can ask myself if I feel I have met the intent of this statement, and at the end of each day before I go to sleep I answer "yes."

So having this life's purpose statement has enabled me to consistently feel that sense of pride, accomplishment, and fulfillment that used to be missing in my life. Even though I may not have accomplished any of my major individual goals that day, if I accomplished just a portion of my life's purpose, my overarching mission, then I met some of my success criteria, and all of a sudden my day was a success.

For example, maybe I had a bad day at work, but I was a loving husband because I spent an incredible evening with my wife just snuggling on the couch and talking or watching a great movie (guys, here's a tip for you: in this situation a great movie means a romantic comedy). Perhaps I was a caring father who took the time to really listen to my daughter or son about something important to them. Maybe I did an extraordinary job of teaching a group of people and knew deep down that I was able to connect with and help some of them in an area they were struggling to understand. Any of these scenarios meet my success criteria and allow me to give myself a pat on the back for a job well done.

You see, having a life's purpose, a mission statement, is truly the fabric of a wonderful life. It is like an artfully crafted tapestry. The supportive goals you develop are woven into your life's purpose like the individual threads that make up a tapestry. If the threads are haphazardly placed with little or no thought and in no particular pattern, you end up with something ordinary. In the same manner, if don't have compelling goals or your goals are haphazardly planned you end up with an ordinary life that you may, or may not, be satisfied with.

On the other hand, if you take your time, plan, and place the threads in just the right manner, you end up with an extraordinary piece of art; something that gives you and others a sense of enjoyment, pride, and accomplishment. Likewise, if you carefully plan your goals to support your life's purpose, your life plan, you will end up with an incredibly rich and extraordinary life that allows you to consistently experience all of the emotions that you designed it to.

People who have a vision of their desired end state and a plan for how they are going to accomplish their goals create masterpieces. Michelangelo didn't just hammer and chip away at a piece of marble without a vision and a plan and end up with a beautiful sculpture. He knew exactly what he wanted and how he was going to accomplish it before he began. He is credited with saying at one point the sculpture was already inside of the block of marble and all he did was chip away the excess pieces. When you think about it, that's true but it would be more accurate to say that the sculpture was inside his mind. He knew exactly what his desired end state was. That is a key concept in this process.

Your life can be a work of art in progress if you want it to. Every day you can look back at your accomplishments and, like Michelangelo looked at his sculpture of The David or the frescos of the Sistine Chapel, feel the exhilaration and pride that comes from completing a masterpiece. Don't settle for ordinary when you can have extraordinary!

> *"The greater danger for most of us is not that our aim is too high and we miss it, but that it is too low and we reach it."*
>
> *Les Brown*
>
> *Michelangelo di Lodovico Buonarroti Simoni (1475-1564)*

Chapter 2.1 Exercise:

Defining Your Life's Purpose and Creating a Life Plan

Why are you here? What is the purpose of your life? In order to define your life's purpose you have to know what's important to you.

To find out what's important to yourself, simply ask questions. The answers will vary greatly from one person to another, and self-honesty is important here. After completing this exercise you may find that you didn't know yourself as well as you thought. In fact, if you ask someone you think you know well to do the same exercise, you may find out that you didn't know him/her as well as you thought.

Many people are so busy with their day-to-day existence that they don't ever take the time to do an inventory of what is really important to them in their hearts. They have allowed the mundane tasks of daily life to become important to them. They live to take out the trash, pay the bills, mow the lawn, and wash the car at the expense of the things that are really important.

Here is your chance to think about what is important to you now as well as what you want to be important to you in the future. As you move through different phases in life, you can redo this exercise to update your life's purpose statement. This is your chance, right here and now, to build a solid foundation upon which you can create the life that you desire and deserve.

Here are some questions to ask yourself to help you get started indentifying what's really important to you:

Questions

Timothy M. Ferris

What is really important to me?

Who are the people in my life who really matter to me?

What excites me?

What am I passionate about?

What are some activities that cause me to lose track of time?

What are some activities that I get so focused on I forget to eat?

What would I do if I could do anything?

What emotions do I want to experience every day? This is important because you will experience the emotions that you focus on the most. So make sure that you focus on good emotions, not bad ones.

What do I want to do with my life?

How far do I want to pursue my education?

When do I want to start a family?

What can I do to contribute back to my community and society in general?

How can I make an impact on the lives of people who are important to me?

How can I set the best example for my children?

How do I want people to treat me?

How do I want to treat people?

Where do I see myself in one, three, five, ten and even twenty years from now?

A helpful exercise is to imagine yourself as an older person reflecting on your life and asking yourself, "Is there anything that I feel like I missed out on? Is there something that I would have liked to experience, but didn't?"

After answering these questions you should have a pretty good idea of what is really important to you now. Next, take the things you discovered are important to you and synthesize them into a small paragraph. Work with it until you are comfortable that it addresses those things that are most important to you.

Don't make it something that will take you the rest of your life to achieve. Make it something that you can experience daily to know that you are on the right track and living your purpose each and every day.

Congratulations! You have just defined your life's purpose. You are way ahead of most people and well on your way to living the life that you want, the life of your dreams.

Now let's continue this exercise with the next step, Creating a Life Plan.

Where do you see yourself five years from now? Ten years from now? Twenty years from now? I want you to sit down and think about all of the things that are important to you. Think about what your dream life would look like in five, ten, even twenty years. One thing is certain, barring any unforeseen catastrophe you will arrive in the future five, ten, even twenty years from now.

The real question is, what will your life look like when you arrive?

And the answer is — It will look much like you want it to if you start taking action now to move your life in that direction.

Do you see yourself with a family? What kind of family? How do you interact with each other?

Do you see yourself as an executive? A doctor? A teacher? A senator? A soldier? You can be all of those things and more if you truly apply your God-given abilities that each of us possess.

What is your education level? Can you tango? Do you go to the opera or Broadway?

I want you to develop a picture of what your life looks like at these different stages in the future. During these two exercises you should have accomplished two things. First, you should have a pretty good picture of where you are currently in your life with respect to the life that you really want to live, your dream life. Second, in this last exercise you should have developed a clear picture of what you want your life to look like in the future. Now you have point A and point B. You know where you are and where you want to go. You have identified the gap between where you are and where you want to be. The next step is to design a plan to close the gap. We do that by setting strategic goals that are aligned with and supportive of our life plan.

Developing Compelling Goals That Support Your Life Plan

Ask and It Will Be Given To You; Seek and You Will Find

Designing and achieving goals that are congruent with your life plan is an integral part of creating success. You can have a vision of the life you've always dreamed of, but if your goals don't support that vision you will never reach it, and you will still be unfulfilled. Without an actionable plan for creating the life you want, you will never manifest your dreams. "Setting goals is vital to an individual's success. Successful people have an unshakable belief, passion, and drive because they have an exciting vision of the future." (Klaus, 2001)

Why should we set goals? Goals allow us to create our future in advance. Goals are the single most effective tool for organizing and focusing our thoughts on what is important to us. For most of us, if we examine our lives closely, we will find that in almost every area of our lives (personal, professional, emotional, financial, and relational) there are gaps between where we are and where we would like to be. Goals are the vehicles we can use to close the gaps. Goals are the milestones that lead us to our dreams, to our ultimate chosen destiny!

Hopefully by now you've made some new and powerful distinctions about how important goal setting is and why we should set goals. Now let's look at the goal setting process.

There are many books, audio programs, videos, and live seminar-type workshops that can teach you how to set goals. I encourage you to expose yourself to as many as you can. I learn something new every time I do a goal setting session. I discover new techniques to help me organize the information better or perhaps a new facet of the goal setting process that I had not previously considered, which enables me to bring greater dimension or clarity to my own goals.

Each new goal setting session I do also serves as a review for me. It allows me to review my current goals to assess their stage of attainment and to consider if they are still valid goals. Any way you look at it, it is a beneficial and worthy process. One of my martial arts teachers, James Muro, used to say, "You have to go outside your system (of martial arts) and study other systems to discover the weaknesses within your own system. What you learn ultimately improves your system, and it is your contribution to the system and to future students."

There are several methods available to guide people in achieving their goals. Some methods are better suited for groups and organizations than they are for pursuing personal goals. I developed my goal-setting rules specifically to help individuals achieve their personal goals and dreams. I developed this system using the acronym "POWERFUL." It makes it easier to remember as well as being a great metaphor for setting powerful goals designed to move you closer to your chosen destiny.

Let's take a closer look at my criterions for developing powerful goals. I'm going to use a real world example of earning a college degree to illustrate the various facets of my goal setting system. This is actually one of my current goals, to earn my Master in Business Administration by Dec 2011. You'll see more about that

P.O.W.E.R.F.U.L. *Mind Energy*

specific goal in the practical exercises. This goal may, or may not, apply to you. Nevertheless, my purpose is to demonstrate to you the completeness and effectiveness of the system so you can apply it to any of your goals. Goals should be:

1. *Purposefully and Autonomously Designed.* Each goal you develop should directly support your overall life plan and be congruent with your life's purpose to move you in the direction of your chosen destiny. For example, part of your life plan should include continuing your education in a field of interest to you. If it doesn't already, I encourage you to add this to your plan. Continuing education should be a top priority for everyone. The world is changing at a dizzying rate, and you have to grow with it or you will be left behind.

    New technologies are altering how we do just about everything from interacting socially with people to planning our vacations to defending our country. I want you to resolve that you are going become a lifelong learner, and one of your goals should address achieving the next level of your education to springboard you to a higher goal that will take you to the next level.

    Another important concept directly related to your chances of successfully achieving your goal is autonomy. Autonomy, as it is used here, means that the goal you set is in line with your personal desires and values as opposed to a goal that you set because of social pressures or expectations of what someone else thinks you should do.

    Studies have shown that the role of autonomy in goal setting is an important factor and impacts greatly an individual's ability and desire to achieve their goals. Goals that are set with a high degree of autonomy have a greater success rate. Koestner (2008) points out that recent research indicates that setting goals autonomously leads to individuals exerting more effort, experiencing less conflict, and a greater sense of readiness to change their behavior in an effort to achieve their goals.

For example, if you want to earn a college degree because you want to learn more about an area that you are passionate about, or you feel that it will make you more successful in your chosen career field, you are much more likely to achieve your goal. Conversely, if you set a goal to go to college primarily because of some external force (i.e. your parents, spouse, boyfriend, girlfriend, or significant other wants you to earn a degree) you are much more likely to fail because you were pressured into setting the goal.

2. *Objectively Assessed.* Each goal you set should be objectively assessed for attainability and risk. You should evaluate your goals as dispassionately as you can to accurately assess their attainability and identify and consider the risks involved. There is a level of risk involved in everything we do. The task here is not to eliminate risk, but to identify and control it.

Remember the old adage, the greater the risk, the greater the potential reward? That is true, but consider the converse of that; the greater the risk the greater the potential loss. If the level of risk seems to be unacceptable, but you are still determined to pursue that goal, try reframing it or breaking it down into smaller goals with more manageable risks.

Continuing with the previous example, is it possible for you to earn a college degree? Absolutely! If I did it as an eighth grade drop-out then anyone can do it. It's just a matter of personal desire and a workable strategy. Are there risks involved? Sure, but there are no risks that cannot be identified, assessed, and controlled.

3. *Well Defined and Measurable.* It is important that you have a clear, well-defined picture of your goal to include what it is, why it is important, and how you will achieve it. Clarity allows you to articulate to your mind exactly what is important to you. <u>The more clearly you define your goals, the greater your chances of success.</u> This principle is based on the fact that it's more difficult to know when you've succeeded if you don't clearly know what you want.

The ability to measure your progress while pursuing a goal is important. This can easily be accomplished by including ways to quantify your progress. Let's continue with the example of earning a college degree. There are several ways to add measurability to this goal. We can measure our progress using grades, number of credit hours, and courses completed. Those metrics considered along with how quickly you want to complete your degree can be used as your yardstick. Almost all programs have a course map that outlines what courses you need to take and a recommended course path. All you have to do is keep up with the program. By adding these dimensions of grades, credit hours, courses taken, we can easily identify intermediate targets, which represent reasonable progress that we can readily track.

Here's our example: "I will earn my undergraduate degree in four years by studying as a full-time student, taking at least twelve credit hours per semester and I will maintain at least a 3.7 GPA and will complete my degree by May 20X4." Now I have a more accurate means to measure my progress. I have set intermediate goals of twelve credit hours per semester along with performance measures in the form of the grades I expect to achieve. These extra dimensions allow me to accurately track my progress on more frequent terms. It is also a control measure that provides me with an indicator of my progress, which allows me to quickly identify short falls and take corrective action in a timely fashion.

4. *Emotionally Anchored.* This is the fuel that drives you to accomplish your goals. What is your motivation to achieve this goal? Why is this so important to you? You must have compelling reasons if you want to achieve your goals. Making your dreams come true takes effort, and it will be difficult at times. You will run into barriers, some seemingly insurmountable. People close to you may not believe in your ability to achieve your dreams and goals. How will you overcome these obstacles? The answer lies in emotionally anchoring your goals by associating them with strong enough reasons why you want to achieve them. You must identify existing reasons or create reasons compelling enough to carry you through the toughest times. The stronger your reasons, the more likely you are to stay the course and follow through on your goals. With strong enough reasons, you can accomplish almost anything you set your mind to. We will discuss this in depth in the next chapter and follow it up with a practical exercise.

5. *Realistically Time-bound.* You must develop a timeline for achieving your goals. Developing a realistic timeline is one more way to add measurability to your goals. By setting a suspense date for completing a task, you are articulating to your mind a level of

importance assigned to that task by you. It's easy to let yourself off the hook by telling yourself, "I'll start tomorrow." Well, like the old saying goes, "Tomorrow never comes." The time for action is now!

By creating a timeline for the achievement of your goals, you create pressure, and by sticking to your timeline and taking small incremental steps toward the achievement of your goals you create momentum. Sustained momentum replicates the power of compounding interest in that you have daily successes building upon the previous day's successes. Now that's power!

You have to realistically evaluate your chances of success in the timeframe you have allotted yourself. By utilizing the previous example again, I can say, "My goal of earning an undergraduate degree in four years" is certainly attainable. Conversely, it would not be reasonable for most people, or as attainable, to set a goal of earning an undergraduate degree in two years, although it is possible.

Additionally, you should:

6. Be *Flexible* in your approach or your plan to accomplish a goal. Obstacles are common in the pursuit of goals. Expect them and be ready for them. You must be able to adapt your approach no matter what the obstacle is. The ability to assess a challenge, reframe it if necessary, and develop a solution that enables you to continue to move forward is imperative.

7. Possess an *Unshakeable Faith* in your ability to achieve whatever goal you set. You will encounter people, most of them close to you, who will tell you that you can't do this or that. They may unintentionally attempt to discourage you in an effort to protect you

from failure. Rubbish! With the right intentions, right thoughts, and right actions, you can do it!

8. Possess a *Lust for Life*, a burning desire to manifest your dreams and goals, live life to its fullest, and squeeze every drop of passion, love, and enjoyment out of life. George Bernard Shaw (1856-1950), the great Irish playwright said it best with this quote:

"This is the true joy in life, being used for a purpose recognized by yourself as a mighty one; being a force of Nature instead of a feverish selfish little clod of ailments and grievances complaining that the world will not devote itself to making you happy. I am of the opinion that my life belongs to the whole community, and as long as I live, it is my privilege to do for it whatever I can. I want to be thoroughly used up when I die. For the harder I work, the more I live. I rejoice in life for its own sake. Life is no brief candle to me. It's a sort of splendid torch which I've got to hold up for the moment, and I want to make it burn as brightly as possible before handing it on to future generations."

Incorporate these rules in the development of your goals and you will be well on your way to achieving the life you once only dreamed of.

Here are some other necessary and helpful tips in addition to the above rules. State your goals in the most positive way that you can. Try to wordsmith the result you are after in a positive manner. For example, instead of "I want to lose some weight," say "I want to add health, fitness, and vitality to the feelings that I experience each and every day so that I can enjoy life in its fullest form!"

To do that, "I will achieve my ideal body weight of one hundred seventy pounds in one year by reducing my weight two pounds per month through daily fitness training, an active lifestyle, and healthy eating choices." Notice that I did not say "lose" weight. It is much better to phrase goals so that you are gaining something as opposed to losing something. Mentally, we are more motivated to gain or achieve something than we are to lose, give up, or quit something.

Visualization is just as important in creating clarity with your goals as it is with creating a vision of who and what you want to be and what you want your life to represent. You have to begin with a clear picture in your mind of the result that you are committed to achieving. As mentioned earlier, the more clearly you can create the images of your dreams and goals in your mind, the more likely you are to manifest them into reality. You must define your goals so that your mind knows exactly what you want. It is important to note here that knowing what you want implies that you also know what you do not want. By getting everything you want along with things you don't, the end result may not be something you will be happy with.

Now that you know what you want and you have created strong enough reasons for why you *must* achieve it, the next step is to design the how. To do this you literally map out the milestones that you must accomplish to bring this goal into reality. This is a mental exercise in which you think your way from where you are now to where you want to be with respect to this goal. As you take this mental journey to your goal, jot down notes as to what actions you need to take each step of the way. This becomes the basis for your plan of action. In essence, you are mentally breaking your goal down into achievable steps that can also be used to measure your progress. This will be discussed in chapter 2.5 and will be followed with a practical exercise.

These steps, defining the result (what you want), creating compelling reasons (why you want it), and designing a course of action to achieve it (how you are going to get it) are the three steps that you must take to develop a goal with clarity. This process allows you to clearly articulate to your mind what is important to you, why it is so important, and what actions you need to take to achieve it. Once your brain knows exactly what you want, why you want it, and how you can get it, it will constantly look for ways to move you closer to that goal. You have now effectively programmed your reticular activating system (RAS). By doing this, your mind will, consciously and subconsciously, look for ways to satisfy the requirements you have defined.

Chapter 2.2 Exercise

Developing Compelling Goals That Support Your Life Plan

You already know what's important to you from the last exercise. Now, keeping that in mind, you need to set goals in each area of your life (personal, professional, emotional, financial, and relational) that are aligned with your purpose. I want you to take two or three minutes in each of these areas and write down as many goals as you can think of. This is not the time to consider whether or not you are capable of achieving it or how you will achieve it. This is your Christmas list, so use your inner child's imagination and go for it. I have included some examples of each area to help jumpstart your thinking process.

Personal goals are things that you would like to have or accomplish for the benefit of yourself and others. For two or three minutes write down everything that comes to your mind.

Do you want to learn to ballroom dance?
Do you want to study yoga?
Do you want to learn martial arts?
Do you want to go to college or complete a degree you've started, but haven't finished?
Do you want to take your lady or man on a romantic getaway to Paris or Italy?
Do you want to learn another language?
Do you want to have an expensive wardrobe?
Do you want to buy your dream car?
Do you want to have a gardener, maid, or cook?
What is your dream house?

Do you want to write a book?
Do you want to travel the world?
Do you want to feel more connected to God?
Do you want to contribute more to the community?
Do you want great grades in school?

Professional goals are things you want to accomplish to enhance your career life. For two or three minutes write down everything that comes to your mind.

Do you want to own your own company?
Do you want a promotion in your current work?
Do you want to change jobs?
Do you want a raise in your salary?
Do you want to go back to school to learn a new skill or earn a degree?
Do you want to work from your home?
Do you want to work from anywhere in the world?

Emotional goals are feelings that you want to experience on a consistent basis. For two or three minutes write down everything that comes to your mind.

What feelings do you want to experience on a regular basis? Passion, joy, cheerfulness, happiness, excitement, love, connectedness, significance, adventure.

What feelings do you want to avoid? Fear, anger, discouragement, jealousy, uncertainty, frustration, disappointment, unhappiness.

Financial goals are money goals that you set. For two or three minutes write down everything that comes to your mind.

How much money would you like to earn?
How much money would you like to save in one, three, five, ten, even twenty years?
What percentage of your monthly income would you like to save and invest?
When do you plan to be financially independent?

How much money would you like to contribute to causes that are important to you?
Would you like to learn to invest?
Would you like to learn to day trade?

Relational goals are relationship goals that you set to take your relationships to the next level. For two or three minutes write down everything that comes to your mind.
How is your relationship with your spouse/significant other and what can you do to make it even better?
How is your relationship with your children and what can you do to make it even better?
How is your relationship with your parents and what can you do to make it even better?
How is your relationship with your co-workers and what can you do to make it even better?
How is your relationship with your classmates and what can you do to make it even better?
How is your relationship with your friends and what can you do to make it even better?
Do you want to be more of a giver and less of a taker?

Now you should have a list of potential goals, things that you want to accomplish at some point in your life. I want you to go through your lists and prioritize each one. Select one goal, maybe your most important one, from each list. You should have five goals now, one from each area. Write them down. These are the goals that we will work with throughout the rest of the book.

Personal _____
Professional _____
Emotional _____
Financial _____
Relational _____

Example: Here is one of my current goals from the Personal/ Professional area of my life.

What I want to do:
Complete my graduate education by earning an Executive Masters in Business Administration by December 2011.

In fact, since just after I started writing this book, I've had to balance my family life, my work, and my studies with completing this book. You can follow my progress over the next year just to make sure I didn't back out on my goals. By telling you this, I'm creating even more pressure on myself to go for it.

Developing Mental Leverage and Hardening Your Will

When The Student Is Ready, The Teacher Will Appear!

The subtitle of this chapter is an old Buddhist maxim and a principle that I have found to be completely true. You cannot and will not alter your beliefs until you, the student, are ready. Knowledge can come to you in many forms, but to internalize it and benefit from it, you must first be willing to consider it and, if it makes sense, accept it.

Throughout history there have been several other phrases that have been used to describe this principle. There is the idiom dating back to around the twelfth century and included by John Heywood in his book of proverbs in 1546, paraphrased in modern English: It says, "You can lead a horse to water, but you can't make him drink."

One of my personal favorites is an axiom from a more recent era and a much better known figure today, Henry Ford, who said, "Whether you think you can, or you think you can't — you're right." Think about that statement and the awesome simplicity of it for a minute. This statement tells us that, whether we can accomplish something or not, is largely a matter of personal beliefs. If we think we can accomplish something, that is, we truly believe with all our heart that we can do it, we have a tremendous advantage over someone who does not believe he can accomplish the task. Conversely, if we think we cannot do something, we probably won't be able to muster the will to get it done.

Why is that true? What is the power behind this simple statement? The theory of cognitive dissonance proposes that a person will take necessary actions, be it altering beliefs and values or changing behavioral patterns, to make their thoughts and actions as congruent as possible.

Let me give you a personal example of this. I was addicted to tobacco for many years. I smoked for over twenty years. I knew, like everyone else, that this was a harmful addiction. In fact, I knew much more about the health risks than an average person. I was a Medical Sergeant in the Green Berets. So I had actually seen the effects close up on patients and cadavers. Plus, there is a warning written in plain view on every package that tells of the harmful effects smoking will have on the health of you and those around you. Yet I continued to do it for so many years, even though I knew it was damaging to my health.

Periodically I would attempt to quit, each time failing to achieve my goal. Many years it was my New Year's resolution to quit. I tried every approach available to me including nicotine gum, the patch, and even the smoking cessation medication Bupropion. Nothing seemed to work long-term for me. Over the years and through many failed attempts I developed a defense mechanism through cognitive dissonance. I had not been successful at changing my behavior, so I altered my beliefs to support it.

When people asked why I smoked even though I knew it was bad for me, I would reply with things like, "Everyone hates a quitter." Or "Anyone can quit. It takes a real man to face cancer." I had several of these quick comebacks that I used to keep myself from feeling the pain of failure every time someone reminded me that I was doing something destructive to myself.

In addition, I told myself things like smoking reduces stress, it helps me control my weight, it makes me feel good, etc. By adopting these erroneous beliefs about smoking, I was bringing my beliefs in line with my behavior. Instead, I should have been altering my beliefs to bring them in line with reality and current research to get the leverage I needed to alter my behavior.

Before continuing my story, let's briefly go over the science that supported me being able to quit smoking, a principle in psychology called the pleasure principle. Philosophers and psychologists have theorized, even from early times, that two basic forces drive human behavior. They are the need to avoid pain and the desire to gain pleasure, the theory being that people's minds will do as much as possible to avoid painful experiences and seek out pleasurable ones. I have found this to be a useful way of evaluating my own behavior and creating leverage on myself to increase my motivation to achieve my goals.

An understanding of this principle, pain and pleasure, will allow you to alter your behaviors by manipulating your belief systems, which is nothing more than changing your thoughts, the way you think about things. This principle can be used to help identify why you behave certain ways now and to instill new empowering beliefs that lead to more desired behaviors.

There are a couple of possibilities that I want to discuss here. The first is that you have some undesirable behavioral traits that you wish to eliminate. The second is that there are some desirable behavioral traits that you want to inculcate in your future behavior.

In the first scenario, if you want to modify your current behavior, perhaps eliminate an undesirable behavioral trait, then evaluate it from the perspective of what pain your present behavior is causing you to experience and what pleasure it is causing you to miss out on. What are all of the bad things, such as negative feelings and outcomes, that you are bringing into your life because of your current behavior?

The key here is self-honesty. First you need to acknowledge that you currently behave in ways that are causing you to experience negative effects. Then you need to identify what those negative effects are and intensify them in your mind. How do you do this? One way is by making big, intense, undesirable, and ugly pictures in your mind and link those pictures to your undesired behavior. To create lasting change in your behavioral patterns, you have get massive amounts of mental leverage on yourself by identifying and becoming consciously aware of all of the pain your current behavior is causing you to experience and also all of the pleasure that it is causing you to miss out on.

By associating these negative feelings with your behavior, this will cause your mind to look for ways to avoid experiencing that pain, and it will be receptive to new behavioral patterns, ones that will enable you to gain pleasure. Then implement your new, desired behavior to fill the void you just created.

In the second scenario, you realize that there are positive and empowering behavioral patterns that you would like to inculcate into your daily routine. Here you are not eliminating a behavioral pattern, you are creating, or installing, a new positive one.

For example, you want to take your relationship with your spouse, girlfriend/boyfriend, or life partner to the next level. To accomplish this, you want to begin to show them that they are special to you more often than you currently do. Maybe now you treat them special or give them gifts only on special occasions. With your new behavior, you decide that you are going to do something, at least one thing, each and every day to let them know how special they are, be it a hug and a kiss, leaving a thoughtful note, a text, a phone call, flowers, fixing a nice dinner, etc.

To make this new behavior stick, again you need to get mental leverage on yourself. You need to focus on all of the pleasure that you will get from this new behavior. Think of all the wonderful and joyful moments you will share with each other. Also, think about the pain you will experience if you fail to do this. Think about all of the wonderful things you will never be able to experience unless you adopt this new behavior. I guarantee you, following through on this simple exercise with that someone special will take your relationship to the next level.

Ultimately, for me to quit smoking, I needed to change my beliefs about smoking. I had to replace my then erroneous beliefs, which I developed to support my destructive behavior, with new beliefs designed to support the behavior I wanted to instill. To do that, I associated massive amounts of pain with my unwanted behavior and massive amounts of pleasure with my desired new behavior I wanted to develop.

When my daughter, Kristina, was about four or five years old, she knew smoking was a bad thing to do. She would find my cigarettes and throw them in the trash every chance she got. In fact, I used my daughter to create much of the mental pressure and leverage I needed to eventually quit. I created mental images of all the bad things that smoking would ultimately lead to, things like images of me walking around with an oxygen bottle to treat emphysema and dying an early death from one of the many diseases associated with smoking.

I love my daughter, and I kept telling myself that I wanted to be around for her as long as I could and that using tobacco was a thief that was slowly stealing my existence from me, which ultimately meant taking time away from me that could be spent with her. She is precious to me, and this created an enormous amount of mental pressure to alter my behavior. By changing my beliefs about smoking, to bring them in line with research and reality, I was then able to change my behavior and quit smoking to bring my behavior in line with my new beliefs.

Once I had solidly changed my beliefs to represent using tobacco bad, quitting tobacco good, my behavior just followed. At the time, my morning ritual was to get a cup of coffee and go outside to have a cigarette. One morning I picked up my pack of cigarettes and I looked at them and thought, I don't even have the urge to smoke a cigarette. Picking them up was just muscle memory, a habit.

I put them back down and went on about my daily routine. It has been thirteen years and I haven't smoked a cigarette since then. In fact, I haven't even had the urge to smoke one. I don't have to avoid situations where I once felt the urge to use tobacco because I'm worried that I may be tempted to smoke, although I do avoid them because I know the harmful effects of second hand smoke. I still occasionally find myself in an area where people are smoking, but I don't have the urge to smoke. My new beliefs are that strong. That's the power of ME: Mind Energy.

You can do the same thing with your mind. You just need to know how to tap into the awesome energy of your mind. The subtitle of this chapter, along with the sayings of John Heywood and Henry Ford, speak directly to a person's individual beliefs, values, and ideals, which are nothing more than thoughts deeply rooted in your mind, thoughts that are usually a result of your past experiences and manifested in your current behavior.

You can, if you are willing, change any of your disempowering beliefs (thoughts) or behaviors to create more empowering ones that better support your life's purpose. You can delete the disempowering ones and replace them with more empowering ones that are aligned with your personal goals. You just have to be willing to listen and learn, and keep an open mind to new ideas no matter how they may conflict with your current beliefs. In doing this it is likely that you will find that some of your current beliefs are actually holding you back. You will also probably find that you have conflicting beliefs. You will need to get rid of those beliefs and develop some new ones that are congruent with your current goals and current life's purpose.

Chapter 2.3 Exercise

Developing Mental Leverage and Hardening Your Will

In the previous chapter you listed as many things as you could think of in two to three minutes for each of the major areas of your life, then you prioritized the list and selected the top priority goal in each area. Let's continue to work on developing these five goals.

The next step is to create pressure by getting mental leverage on yourself for each of these goals. I want you to dig down deep inside yourself and find the reasons you want to achieve these goals. This is where the pleasure principle comes into play. For each goal, list all of the pleasure that achieving that goal will allow you to experience. Then list all of the pain you will experience if you don't achieve these goals.

Do this with as much clarity as you can because the more clearly you can see what you gain and what you will miss out on, the more real it will seem to your mind and the more psychological pressure you will create. Your mind will use this pressure as leverage to look for ways to take action even in the face of difficulty.

Personal_____

_____
Professional_____

_____
Emotional_____

_____

Timothy M. Ferris

Financial_____

_____

Relational_____

_____

Example: I'll continue with my goal from the previous chapter of completing my graduate studies.

Why I want to do it:
What pleasure will I experience?
-Education is the key to life's fulfillment.
-Knowledge empowers me to make actionable decisions.
-Knowledge enables me to give clarity to my goals.
-This will reconfirm my commitment to lifelong learning.
-It will increase my knowledge of business practices.
-It will increase my marketability.
-It will increase my quality of life.
-It will set a positive role model for others, especially my children, Kristina and Nicky.
-It will set me up for my doctorate degree.

Ignorance is not bliss, but rather intellectual paralysis!

What pain will I experience if I don't do this?
-<u>Without knowledge, I am intellectually paralyzed</u> to the point where I feel trapped.
-I cannot take the actions I want because I do not have the skills, knowledge, and abilities required.
-I won't be able to earn my doctorate degree without taking this step first.
-I will miss out on all of the knowledge and experiences that the program offers.
-I will not be able to grow my company to its full potential.
-I will have to live with the fact that I did not put forth my best effort to accomplish one of my goals.

The Incredible Power of Visualization

With Our Thoughts We Make Our World

Every action in your life originates as a thought. Ralph Waldo Emerson, the great American essayist and poet, said, "The ancestor to every action is a thought." Stop now and consider that carefully for a moment. Everything that you have manifested into your life started as a thought.

Think about anything that is in your life now that you once dreamed of and now you have it. As you reflect on this material object, relationship, or state of mind, know that *you made it happen!* You created your life situation, first by your thoughts, followed up with the actions taken that brought those thoughts into your physical world. It doesn't matter if it is a relationship, a car, a house, a job, the latest mobile phone, or a project at work. You made it happen!

> *"We are what we think.*
> *All that we are arises with our thoughts.*
> *With our thoughts we make our world."*
> Buddha (635 BC)

Your ability to focus your thoughts is perhaps the single most powerful skill that you can develop. The more clarity you put into a thought, the more powerful that thought becomes. We think in images like pictures and videos. Our thoughts are really images. Images that are clear and vivid evoke strong emotional responses, and images that are unclear and distant do not evoke strong emotions. That is why when we experience strong emotions immediately after a significant emotional event, good or bad, with time the feelings associated with that event fade. The images associated with it become blurred with time.

We can purposefully control all of the visual aspects of those images. We can make them brighter or darker, high or low contrast, color or black and white. We can even add dialogue and soundtracks if we like. This ability to mentally manipulate the visual aspects of an image in your mind is a powerful tool that can be used to control emotion as well as helping you develop a clear image of who you want to be and what you want your future to look like.

This is a skill and, like any other skill, the more you practice it, the better you become at it. You will want to practice manipulating your mental images until you are good at it. You need to be able to create a thought with such clarity and detail that your mind can't tell the difference between your thoughts and the real thing.

Making your mental images more intense will cause you to experience more intense emotion associated with them. Increasing the intensity of an image comes in handy for those images that evoke a positive emotional response. For example, you can take a relationship to the next level by increasing the intensity of the positive images you have in your mind, then acting on those images. Conversely, by making your mental images less intense, you will decrease the emotional response to them. Your ability to decrease the intensity of your mental images will help you decrease your response to disempowering emotions.

This is not a new concept. This is something that peak performers in many fields have been doing for centuries. Arnold

Schwarzenegger is a big promoter of using visualization techniques in the attainment of goals. Here's what he had to say about visualization:

> "When I was very young, I visualized myself being and having what it was I wanted. Mentally, I never had any doubts about it. The mind is really so incredible. Before I won my first Mr. Universe, I walked around the tournament like I owned it. The title was already mine. I had won it so many times in my mind that there was no doubt I would win it. Then, when I moved on to the movies, the same thing. I visualized myself being a successful actor and earning big money. I could feel and taste success. I just knew it would all happen."
>
> Arnold Schwarzenegger

Your role in life can be passive or active, it's up to you. Your life is all about the choices you make. You can choose to sit by passively *letting life happen to you* or, as Leonardo da Vinci suggested, you can choose to *actively make life happen for you*.

You can sculpt a life that many only dream of by harnessing the incredible power of your mind and taking consistent action. Your mind is the most powerful computer available to you. Learn to use it well by learning how it works and how you can direct its awesome power to work for your greater benefit.

The mind is a powerful tool. It's like a search engine or a sophisticated tracking device. By developing a vision of your life's purpose and setting goals, you are telling your mind what is important to you. You are, in a sense, programming your mind by inputting the search parameters. At that point the mind, like a sophisticated tracking device, takes over and begins to search out its target.

What makes the mind like a sophisticated tracking device? Answer: The reticular activating system (RAS). The RAS is the attention center of the brain. It is a diffuse and complex part of the brain which is the center for arousal and motivation in mammals. We cannot possibly intake and process the incalculable amount of sensory information from our environment at any given moment. It's the RAS' job to delete information that is unimportant.

How does the RAS know what is and what is not important to us? It's simple; we tell it. We tell the RAS what to focus on with our thoughts. The thoughts that we have often are the one's the RAS interprets as important to us, so it looks for things in our external world that meet the parameters of what we focus on in our mind.

Have you ever seen a car or a new outfit that appeals to you and thought, that is so unique! I don't think I've ever seen that before. I am going to get one of those. And in the days or weeks that follow you are seeing them everywhere. All of a sudden they are not so unique. Why is that? Did they not exist until you saw them a week or two ago? No, they probably existed and were just as prevalent; they just weren't important to you then. You had not told your RAS that they were important, so it automatically deleted them from your sensory intake.

> "The Reticular System is the attention center in the brain. It is the key to 'turning on the subconscious capabilities of our creative mind.' Many believe it to be the center of motivation. The Reticular Activating System determines what we pay attention to. In other words, it is the part of your brain where the world 'outside' of you and your 'inside' world of thoughts and feelings come together and meet." (Jim Henion, 2001).

I hope that the information presented in this chapter has convinced you of the importance of being able to clearly visualize your life's purpose and your goals. To experience the power of your mind and thought, you must first tell your mind what is important to you. You need to have a mental map, a visual image that tells your mind where you want to be. Then, with two firm reference points, where you are now and where you want to be in the future, you can plot a course to your dreams.

You don't have to wait until some sign comes to you from beyond. You can define the purpose of your life right now. It doesn't matter if it changes later. Later, you will be a different person than the one you are now. You can adjust your life's purpose as you grow, make new distinctions, and refine your life skills.

You have to have a purpose in order to experience that sense of pride, accomplishment, and fulfillment that can only come from knowing that every day you are doing something to move yourself in the direction of your chosen purpose. It also serves as the device through which you can measure your progress. To measure anything you must have at least two reference points. You can't measure your life's progress unless you have defined your current state and developed an end-state.

Chapter 2.4 Exercise

The Incredible Power of Visualization

In the previous chapter's exercise, you used the pleasure principle to create mental pressure on yourself by coming up with lots of reasons why you must take action to achieve your goals.

In this chapter's exercise, I want you to work on developing your ability to visualize yourself living your life's purpose and achieving your goals. I want you to create and manipulate mental images in your mind of your goals completed. As mentioned earlier, the more clearly you can see what you want to accomplish in your mind, the more likely you are to manifest it in your physical world. This may sound a bit metaphysical, but on a simpler level you must know what your end state is to have the best chance of achieving it. This principal applies to virtually everything you do.

Creating images in your mind is like any other skill; the more you practice it, the better you become at it. In the digital age it is now easier than ever for someone to learn this skill. With the invention of digital images and image manipulation software, there are lots of solid references that most people today can relate to with regard to image manipulation. All you have to do is apply the same techniques to images in your mind. You can zoom in to make an experience more intense or zoom out to make it far away and insignificant. You can increase and decrease contrast, make colors more vivid or black and white, erase or clone specific areas, and cause images to fade in and out. You can even add a soundtrack to affect the mood of the viewer, you.

You have control over the way you perceive external events in your mind. You don't have control over the external events themselves. Events that prompt you to create vivid, colorful, close-up, and loud pictures evoke strong emotions. You can use this to your advantage by associating strong emotions with your goals. You need to create vivid, colorful, and close-up pictures with motivating audio associations to tap into useful and empowering emotions like passion, love, motivation, persistence, adventure, happiness, joy, gratitude, etc.

Your exercise is to use your powers of visualization to create empowering images for each of your goals. Keep these images in your mind and refer to them often, making them clearer, brighter, and bigger until you have manifested them into your physical world.

This is a technique that has been used by many people for some time now to produce peak results. It is particularly popular in the athletic world. Don't just take my word for it. Do some quick research, and you will find that visualization techniques are an integral part of achievement for many highly successful people. Remember Arnold Schwarzenegger's quote?

Example: Continuing with my example to complete my graduate studies, I use my visualization techniques to see myself succeeding each step of the way. I already have the degree in my mind. I can see myself working with my classmates and professors, collaborating on team projects, and touring companies on the international study trip. I can hear my name being announced and see myself walking across the stage on Commencement Day. I can feel the excitement that comes from striving to accomplish a challenging goal and triumphing.

Taking Action Now and Consistently Following Through

Courage Has Genius, Power, And Magic In It

Now that you have chosen a purpose and developed an exciting life plan with a set of compelling and powerful goals using all of the techniques discussed in the previous chapters, it's time to create momentum by taking consistent action in the direction of those goals and the direction of the life you've dreamed of.

Your goals are just a lot of words written on paper and images in your mind unless you discipline yourself to take action that results in regular progress toward their achievement. That means keeping your goals in the forefront of your mind and taking some form of action every day that moves you closer and closer to accomplishing your goals. There are lots of ways you can do this.

For starters, it is important to review your goals regularly. That will keep them fresh in your mind and constantly reinforce the message to your RAS that they are important. Remember this, the difference between daydreaming and achieving your dreams is action. Daydreamers are great at developing mental images of how they want their life to be, just not so great about taking action. So, if you are good at daydreaming, that's great! What I want you to do is push through the daydreaming stage into the action stage. That's where all great achievers are. They are achievers precisely because they take action on their thoughts, the images they create in their minds.

Developing a plan of action and following through on it is the only way to achieve success. You should develop goals that support your life plan and develop intermediate steps, or milestones, that support achieving your goals.

Think about the goals you decided to pursue in Chapter 2.2. For each of those goals you need to develop an actionable plan for how you are going to achieve each one. Begin by mentally accomplishing the goal in a step-by-step fashion from start to finish. Write down or type out the sequential process that you need to complete to achieve your goal. A computer works best for this since you can easily add, delete, and insert text as necessary. Start out with broad-brush strokes by outlining the major steps you need to accomplish. Then, drill down into each step, identifying the sub-steps and sub-sub-steps.

In the exercise at the end of this chapter I include my action plan for earning my Master's degree to give you an example of the level of detail that I use in creating an action plan for all of my goals. My action plan is one of my control measures because I can use it to track my progress against the milestones that I have put in place to accomplish that goal. It also provides me with motivation each time I complete one of the steps because I know I'm getting closer and closer to achieving my goal and that motivation creates momentum.

In business there is a concept called *Kaizen*, a Japanese term for "improvement" or "change for the better." In business, this refers to a system of continuous improvement or change for the better. The changes can be big, but often they are small incremental changes that alone would be insignificant. However, when the effects of these seemingly insignificant changes are stacked upon one another, the end results can be staggering.

I want you to apply the concept of kaizen to your own life by taking consistent action toward the achievement of your goals. Every day do something that moves you closer to achieving one of your goals. It could be something as simple as making a phone call or doing some quick research on the Internet. You don't have to do something big, just do something!

Keep in mind the parameters you learned in chapter 2.2 and incorporate them into your plan wherever appropriate. Ensure that you set POWERFUL goals:

Purposefully and Autonomously Set
Objectively Assessed for Attainability and Risk
Well-Defined and Measurable
Emotionally Anchored
Realistically Time-Bound
Flexibility in Your Approach
Unshakeable Belief in Your Ability to Achieve
Lust for Life or Burning Desire to Achieve

Maintaining awareness of your progress allows you to assess where you are in relation to achieving your individual goals and your overall vision of your life's purpose. To stay on task, you have to keep your eye on the prize and continually assess your progress. To do this, I recommend reviewing your top goals daily. By reviewing your top goals daily, each day you are renewing your commitment to achieving them and you are telling yourself what is most important to you. As you go about your daily business you will consciously look for ways to move closer to your goals. And your mind, through your reticular activating system (RAS), will subconsciously look for ways to move you closer to the achievement of your goals.

If you review your goals and realize that you haven't taken action toward the achievement of a specific goal in several days, you can renew your commitment to take action. Reading your goals daily allows you to assess which steps you have achieved and whether or not you are hitting your timelines. If you find you are consistently not hitting your timelines, you should consider whether they are realistic. Just because you are not consistently hitting your timelines and making progress like you planned doesn't mean that your goal is not achievable. You may have been overly aggressive in your initial time estimates, and it may only require that you adjust your timelines. Some of my goals have taken me many years to fully realize.

As you can see, reviewing your goals regularly produces positive benefits at multiple levels. Something as simple as checking off the intermediate steps completed to date is a visual indicator of progress. It is an indicator of progress and success, and it will motivate you to take even more action in the future. There is nothing quite as satisfying nor as motivating as making a simple check mark next to the goals or intermediate steps you have completed. It is a physical acknowledgement that you are doing what you said you would do, and you are making progress in the direction of your dreams.

Sometimes while reviewing a goal you may find that an intermediate step, or maybe the entire goal, is no longer appropriate. That's okay. We set the goals, and we can alter or delete them if they no longer support our overall plan. Changing a goal that is no longer appropriate is not the same as giving up on a goal. Don't feel bad if you come to a place in your life where one of your goals is no longer valid because it no longer supports your life plan. We are constantly growing and changing, and our life plan must be updated to support this. So maybe, based on where you are in life now, climbing Mount Everest is no longer that important. Maybe just going to base camp will be accomplishment enough.

In this book I have only briefly touched on the enormous amount of information now available on goal setting and peak performance techniques. It is my hope that the information presented has provoked profound and sustained thought in each of you with regard to what you are capable of accomplishing simply by harnessing and focusing your mind's energy. My purpose was to educate you to the awesome possibilities of life that are available to each and every one of us and a practical method for accessing those possibilities. We each have a mind and the potential of our minds is much more powerful than most people have ever imagined.

> "Optimal human functioning requires the courage to live with realness and purpose, rather than merely enduring a life of mindless conformity, insecurity, and fear. Acting on courage and taking risks are necessary to meet needs, fulfill desires, resist fears, contribute to society, and to avoid the alternative – living a passionless, ineffective, and narrow life."
> (Griffith, 2004)

Remember, it is first with our minds that we make our dreams come true. As we learn, grow, and make better distinctions about life, we may alter our dreams and the goals that support those dreams. Just as we are each the sum total of all of our past thoughts and actions, likewise at any given point in the future we will each be the sum total of all of our thoughts and actions between now and that point. So, don't procrastinate. The time to create your future is now!

> "Lose this day loitering, 'twill be the same story
> Tomorrow, and the rest more dilatory;
> Thus, Indecision brings its own delays And days are lost lamenting over days, Are you in earnest?
> Seize this very moment; What you can do, or
> Dream you can, begin it.
> Courage has genius, power, and magic in it;
> Only engage, and then the mind grows heated.
> Begin it, and the work will be completed."
> -Johann Wolfgang Von Goethe *(1749-1832)*

Chapter 2.5 Practical Exercise

Taking Action Now and Consistently Following Through

Now you need to develop a solid plan for how you are going to achieve your goals and take consistent action toward their achievement. Gather as much information as you can about your goal and what it will take to manifest it. Develop a step-by-step plan that is thorough, yet flexible, enough to allow you the greatest chance of success. Remember to use all of the parameters of a well-developed goal outlined in Chapter 2.2.

Here is my action plan for earning my Master's degree. This should give you a good idea of the level of planning that I do for all of my goals. I don't just list the big steps. I list the little ones, too, because by completing even the smallest of steps, it boosts my confidence in my ability to achieve my goals, and it is a positive visual indicator that I am moving in the right direction.

<u>Plan of Action</u>: How will I achieve this goal?

1. Contact prestigious universities that offer online education and MBA programs
    1.1 Identify programs of interest: UT at Dallas, Duke, and Georgetown
    1.2 Go online and get contact info.
    1.3 Call and get enrollment information.
2. Obtain financing

2.1 Apply to the VA now for the Post 9/11 Education Assistance Program. Awarded 70% educational expenses by the VA!
2.2 Follow-up with VA.
2.3 Research other options for financial aid options.
    2.3.1 Federal Student Loans: Applied and approved!
    2.3.2 Grants: Look for grants.
    2.3.3 Scholarships: Look for scholarships.

3. Apply in the selected universities in time to be accepted for the Spring 2010 term: Accepted in University of Texas at Dallas Global Leadership Executive MBA program!
   3.1 Identify all entrance requirements: This week
      3.1.1 Application Process:
         3.1.1.1 Application sent
         3.1.1.2 Three Letters of Recommendation: Done
         3.1.1.3 Complete essay and submit: Done
         3.1.1.4 Employer Letter of Understanding: Done
         3.1.1.5 Submit all transcripts from previous universities: Done
      3.1.2 GMAT: Not Required for GLEMBA
      3.1.3 Develop career goals for letters and interviews: Done

4. Enroll in the selected university and complete my degree: Enrolled in UT at Dallas!
   4.1 Complete all courses by Dec 2011.

5. Master's Degree Complete!

6. Move on to the Doctoral Degree Program and continue learning, growing, and contributing!
   6.1 Decide on a Doctoral Program

6.2 Decide on University and contact them about enrollment.
6.3 Enroll and continue learning!
6.4 Identify possible financial aid vehicles.

REFERENCES

Griffith, B. A. (2004). Meeting Needs and Making Meaning; The Pursuit of Goals. *The Journal of Individual Psychology: 60* (1), 25-41.

Henion, J. (2001, June 18) *Why Goal Setting Works*. Retrieved February 6, 2009, from http://documents.crinet.com/CRI-Corporate/Sales-Training/goalset.pdf

Klaus, P. (2001). Winning Goals. *Professional Engineering: 14* (3), 61.

Koestner, R. (2008). Reaching One's Personal Goals: A Motivational Perspective Focused on Autonomy. *Canadian Psychology: 49* (1), 60-67.

Robbins, A., Personal Power. CD-ROM. Disk 2. Classic Edition. San Diego, CA: Robbins Research International, 1993,1996.

Robbins, A., Get The Edge. CD-ROM. Disk 7. San Diego, CA: Robbins Research International, 2000.

Robbins, A. (1991). Awaken the Giant Within: How to Take Immediate Control of Your Mental, Emotional, Physical, and Financial Destiny! New York: Free Press

SUCCESS NOTES

SUCCESS NOTES

SUCCESS NOTES

SUCCESS NOTES

SUCCESS NOTES